Confessions of a Priest

By Jim Koepke

Books by Jim Koepke

Adventures in a Mental Health Center – A novel that offers a revealing look at the state of mental health services.

Chasing Ghosts – A nonfiction study about the assassination of President Kennedy.

My North Korea Vacation – A historical novel about an attempt by American special forces to destroy North Korean nuclear weapons.

Cover Photo – by Jane Moisio

This book is dedicated to the Catholic priests of the world. God bless you for dedicating your lives to serving God. My hope is that this book will entertain the reader while educating about the busy, productive and necessary work priests do every day.

A special dedication goes to Fr. Thomas Stack who allowed an eight-year-old me to participate in my first Holy Communion even though I had broken the required fast right before Mass started. My mother had left some candy out for the celebration afterward and, well, I was eight years old. Fifty years later I still cannot be trusted with a bowl of candy.

Disclaimer: This book is a novel. All characters within are figments of an unceasingly overactive imagination. While there is no disputing that I have known, worked with, and endlessly annoyed countless priests during my life, the ones written about here are fictional.

FORWARD

The priest of the Catholic Church is an endangered man. A man who commits his life to God should be celebrated. Priests are highly intelligent, well-educated and tireless workers. These traits would serve them well financially had they chosen other careers. We are fortunate priests have chosen to turn away from material rewards to embrace spiritual ones. Yet the media focuses not on our good fortune to have these extraordinary men at our service – it focuses on those very few who have betrayed their vows to God. It is time to take back the priesthood and reinforce the truth – that the world is a far better place with priests than it would be without them.

This book is a love story about a priest. The Catholic Church, the institution begun by Jesus, is the love of this priest's life. When faced with challenges, he turns them over to God and encourages his parishioners to do the same. The joyous results of his work are written here.

This story is meant to be entertaining while encouraging serious thought and discussion about the magnificent priests who serve us.

Preface

Journal Entry #1. First of many.

Last Christmas my mother gave me a journal. A journal is what she called it. It is in reality a diary. She gave a grown, fifty year old man a diary. Growing up, I knew lots of people who had diaries. All of them were teenage girls. Thanks, Mom.

When I asked her – as gently as I could, after all, I am a priest – why she gave me such a gift, she told me something as ridiculous as it was incredible.

Mom told me that writing was therapy.

Therapy? I cannot begin to relate how upset I was by that comment. This no doubt well-meaning comment led Mom to try to calm me down. She told me that she saw the stress I lived with every day. She believed that writing my thoughts down each day would provide some sort of cleansing of my soul. Or conscience. Or some damn thing, I don't know.

So, being a good son (though probably a mediocre priest), I graciously thanked her and promised I would make good use of the diary – I mean journal. Six months later, when mom was cleaning my room – yes, that is right, my mother cleans my room, I will explain more about that later – she stumbled upon my unused, unopened journal lying in the bottom of my closet.

Now having been caught and proven an ungrateful son, I have no choice but to begin writing. While I cannot imagine what I will find to say, I will proceed to make use of this book. My intention is that no one besides me and perhaps my long-suffering guardian angel will ever read these pages of private revelation. However, if anyone does make the error of checking out these jottings, please note that one of my many flaws is I find humor in most everything. Sometimes my humor is so subtle (or maybe unfunny) that it comes across as crass or mean-spirited. So please remember that if any of my writings seem a bit over the top, it is just my lack of ability to put words together in a manner that amuses you, reader, as much as myself. I will not use dates, as one day runs into another in my profession. When a series of dates has together become another chapter in my life, I will so note it. Yes, I will begin to use the journal. But not today. I am tired and want to get a good night's sleep. So, beginning tomorrow morning, the gloves come off and my thoughts go in. I am certain that the first thing I write will be a theological statement of such magnitude that the heavens themselves will quiver.

CHAPTER ONE

"I damn you. I damn you to hell unless you quiet down now!" My priestly exhortation was stern and loud. It did no good. The alarm clock kept ringing. My vain attempt to condemn the wretched dream destroyer had failed. Making silly jokes like this made me feel good about myself, even if I was the only one who heard them. When you are not married, you better be able to enjoy your own company, and I did. Lack of humility, a sin if ever there was one, held me firm.

I reached over to the clock all the while trying not to remove my tired fifty-year-old body from my bed.

Twenty-five years as a priest meant I should have the right to sleep in once in a while. I turned the alarm off then rolled over and shut my eyes. Drifting waves of happy slumber re-embraced me. But it was not to last.

THUMP, THUMP, THUMP. My bedroom door reverberated from the pounding of a heavy hand.

"Johnny!" my mother shouted. "Johnny, are you awake? Did you forget the Bishop will be here in an hour?"

Fifty years old and I still had my mother acting as my alarm clock and telling me how to live. "Honor thy Father and Mother." God must have been thinking of me when He wrote that.

I sat up in my bed, leaned over, and pulled up the shades. The clouds were so thick only the faintest light shone on the church steeple. I remember years ago, when I first became a priest, I would look out and watch the sun rise each morning. The magnificent glow from those golden rays shone brightly on that spire. Watching it would invigorate me and cause me to fly out of bed every morning. Oh, how I looked forward to each and every day. Perhaps it is inevitable that things change. As the years passed by the steeple grew tarnished. Every so often I considered cleaning it. Contractors gave us bids which were far more than our budget would allow. It was too dangerous to ask my parishioners to attempt climbing that tower to clean it. That left me. I was not a fearful man. I was not afraid of anyone, at least not since I punched the school bully in junior high. Heights, though, terrified me. It wasn't something I was proud of but I believed everyone was allowed some unconquerable barrier in their life. Besides, I enjoyed my comfort and not climbing up that steeple kept me feeling very comfortable, very comfortable indeed.

Today, I embraced my comfort and closed my eyes while pulling the blankets over my head. I knew the Bishop was going to be here at 8:30. A timely man, he would arrive five minutes early. Bishop Kevin O'Reilly could only be described by utilizing a long list of positive adjectives. He was holy – no question about that. Intellectually he was gifted far beyond anyone I knew. Theologically, he had achieved a level of excellence I could not approach. The Bishop's dedication to the Catholic Church was admirable. He also was my nemesis. Okay, I am kidding about the nemesis label. The Bishop brought out the best in me by constantly challenging me. It is doubtful I returned the favor.

I have always believed that the best relationships are those that nurture a lot of vibrant conversation. A style of friendly debate with give and take, back-and-forth dialogue, encourages deep thought. My family engaged in lively debates while I grew up. Politics, sports, and of course religion were all subjects were would discuss with fun and gusto. As I left the nest I found others did not enjoy the form of discussion I did. Unfortunately, I have had trouble changing. It has taken a lot of work on my part to watch what I say to folks – all the more important because of my profession. I fear more people have left the faith due to a stray comment from their parish priest than because of a loss of faith.

After this marathon of thoughts cleared through my head I checked the clock. I now had fifty-five minutes to eat, shave, shower, and dress. I could do it in forty-five. Except I had not yet said my rosary. Prayer brought me to God and brought me peace and contentment, much unlike my time with the Bishop. A quick rosary would still give me thirty-five minutes to prepare myself to meet with my nemesis. Oh, no. I used that word again. No matter. One of my few secrets is that I enjoyed pushing myself to the limit. I pulled my six foot frame up and looked at myself in the mirror. Where had the years gone? I had gained a little weight over the years but still looked fairly lean. The hair, though, was another thing. My thick, dark hair had thinned a little and most of the strands remaining had turned white. Oh, how I treasured the few remaining brown wisps of hair. Here I was a priest, but just like any other middle aged man, struggling with vanity.

With ten minutes to spare I sat myself down for coffee and eggs. My mother gave me her most disapproving look as she served up the food.

"Cutting it a little close, aren't you, Johnny?" she said with a small dose of concern in her voice. By the time I turned twelve I had figured out that Mom was pushover. Approaching seventy-two years of age, she remained the energetic, cheerful woman who used to put up with my temper tantrums and help me with my homework. Her tough talk was a façade, but I pretended to be impressed by it.

"Well, I probably won't keep His Eminence waiting more than twenty minutes." I knew this would warm up the conversation.

"Bishop O'Reilly is a busy man and deserves your total respect," Mom instructed me. "He is your leader."

"I have only one leader on earth and he lives in Vatican City. Or were you speaking of God?" I softly countered, pointing upward.

"Remember the fourth commandment, Father John." Mom was doing her best to make her voice sound icy though her warm loving manner never could be overruled. I would, as always, call her bluff.

"I haven't killed anyone," I playfully responded. "Oh, wait, the *fourth* commandment. Honor thy father and mother. I get the order mixed up sometimes." I glanced out of the corner of my eye to make sure my silliness was having the desired effect.

"You remind me of your father. But not in a good way." A slight smile and a pat on the shoulder topped off a perfect touché from the woman who knew me best.

Five years ago my father happened to die the same week my housekeeper retired. The Bishop suggested I hire Mom and move her into the house. At the time I appreciated it because I thought he was trying to console the two of us by having us live together. Lately, I wonder if he just wanted someone to keep me in line. That was the last time I took His Eminence's advice about anything.

"You know what, it is eight-thirty and he hasn't arrived. Maybe he isn't coming," I said, with hope in my voice.

"He is such a dear man." She was on his side, no doubt about it. I was expected to be also. Alas, I never ceased to disappoint.

"Maybe you should meet with him instead of me," I offered.

Mom pretended to ignore me. "I have plenty to do today. The bedrooms need to be dusted and vacuumed."

"Why"?

"Haven't you heard that cleanliness is next to Godliness?"

There was no point in reasoning with the woman. Why anyone would spend time cleaning rooms that were never used was beyond me. Seventy-five years ago when the Diocese purchased this house they needed a home for five priests. The number of priests have dwindled over the decades and now the only people who lived here were mom and me. That meant three bedrooms stood empty. But mom still kept them as clean as if they might be used any day.

“Oh, good!” Mom exclaimed. I knew what the happiness in her tone meant. “His car pulled into the driveway.”

I took one more bite of my food and walked to the front door.

“Kevin, how are you? Please come in.” I greeted him as best I could. The Bishop was a good man. He was much more learned than me and worked very hard. Something about him brought out my healthy disrespect for authority. It was easy to be intimidated by the Bishop’s physical presence. At least a half foot taller than me and retaining an athletic build, even though he was in his mid-sixties, he was an imposing figure. An imposing physical presence never meant much to me. Ever since I knocked school bully Joey Jones on his butt in ninth grade I had lost the ability to be intimidated by anyone, even my Goliath-like boss. Reflecting back, it was good to get the willingness to fight out of me at a young age. Thankfully, that was my first and last physical confrontation. It would not do for a priest to walk around town pounding on people.

I welcomed the Bishop into the living room. Mom had left a pot of coffee and I poured him a cup. Not forthcoming by nature, he seemed to be withholding something. But patience was a virtue I didn't have.

"So, John, how are things going at St. Jude?" He started off with the usual pleasantries.

"Everything here is fine. So I guess now you'll be leaving?" I started to stand while attempting to show an innocent expression on my face.

A very slight smile crossed the Bishop's face.

"Never were one for small talk, were you, John?" The Bishop knew me well.

"Well, Kevin, the fact is I see you about twice a year. And it is always bad news. The last time was about, what, five months ago? Have I told you lately how unsupported I felt by you during that event?" I knew the answer to my question before it came out of my mouth.

The Bishop was a bit surprised by what I asked and responded abruptly, "Surely you did not expect me to ignore a serious complaint about one of my priests? With all that has gone on the last several years I have to take every whisper of scandal seriously."

"And that means following up on every investigation thoroughly, which to me means confronting those who are spewing forth all sorts of vile stories in order to seek some sort of revenge for imagined slights."

"John, that is a very eloquent proclamation, as you are prone to make. I still don't know what you would have had me do differently." The Bishop spoke calmly and plainly.

"Stand up for your priest. Stand up for a priest who has served in this diocese for twenty-five years. Some might say I only ask that you perform your duties as a Bishop." I was a little out of line with that statement but the Bishop knew me well enough to expect frank conversation. He wasn't going to be disappointed.

"You know, John, it has been a long time since I have been at the seminary—a while but less time for you, too. Tell me, when you had classes there did they no longer teach things about how to work with people, especially superiors?" Even when I pushed him, the Bishop still had the class not to lose his temper. This declaration of his was mild compared to what a lot of people would have replied.

"Superiors? I'll pretend I didn't hear that. As far as what they taught when I went to the seminary, it was mostly useless things . . . like theology."

"And let us keep in mind that I have the authority to send you to any mosquito-infested backwater in the Diocese." We enjoyed our dueling, we really did. It was unusual for the Bishop was to play his trump card this early in the game. I ignored his attempt at closure and continued.

"Have you been in the backyard here in July? I'll wager my mosquitoes could take on any in the Diocese."

"And, after all, you are the only priest in the Diocese who has his mother living with him." The Bishop brought this up, I assume, to remind me I had a privileged circumstance. There was no question he had the authority to tell me she would have to find a new home.

“She makes my life a living hell,” I countered, playing to his empathic side.

“In that case she can stay.” The Bishop smiled.

The Bishop folded his hands. I didn’t know if he was going to continue jousting or move on to the reason for his visit. There was no end to the disappointment.

“I appreciate your humor. I am just saying, John, that our encounters are always a bit . . . tense.” Again, the soft smile. The man had a way of disarming one with his nonverbal approach. For all I knew he was a genius. Most of the bishops I have known were. None of that changed the fact that his insinuating himself into my world seldom turned out well for me.

"So getting back to my question," I said, trying to make him uncomfortable so he would move along to his reason for visiting. "You do remember our little get together five months ago? And you wonder why our meetings are uncomfortable?"

The Bishop nodded. He grimaced as memories of that rolled around in his head.

"Yes, you know I didn't want to do it. I only did it because it was my job." What with all the scandals that had gone on in the last several years we needed to err on the side of caution.

"An anonymous person sent you letters stating I was guilty of horrible things. Let's see, she said I was the least holy priest ever to serve."

"Yes, but . . ." The Bishop vainly attempted to quiet me. I was on an unstoppable roll.

“Now,” I admitted, “those accusations were probably correct.” I figured a little honesty never hurt. “But then the lies followed by the damn lies. She said I was having a sexual liaison with not one but several women, was a raging alcoholic, preached from the pulpit that sin was okay and in my spare time had set up a meth lab in the garage.”

“You use the word ‘she,’ and we don’t know the name of the writer or whether it was a man or woman.” The Bishop was drowning and desperately thrashing about looking for a straw to grasp.

“I know who it was. You know who it was. Mrs. Luci Satane is the person who sent the letters.” There was no point to pretending.

“We can’t say with certainty.” The Bishop could not let go of his naiveté.

“We can. Do you remember that day?”

“I do.” The Bishop grew more uncomfortable as the conversation continued.

“You met with me here. After listening to the nonsensical accusation for an hour – wait – the accusation only took a few minutes. What took so long was getting you to the point of your visit. Today shows, if nothing else, that you are consistent. Anyway, back then I asked you to call Mrs. Satane and see if you could stop by her house.”

“I never should have let you talk me into that,” the Bishop muttered regretfully.

“You’d have preferred to think I was guilty?”

“I never thought you were guilty.”

“Ah, the look on Mrs. Satane’s face when she opened the door and saw you. She was so delighted to see you had taken her accusations seriously enough to come over to hear more of her lunacy. Then the look on her face changed when she saw me standing behind you.”

“Go on, “the Bishop sighed. “Get it out of your system.”

“So when we walked into her house I very politely asked her if she had sent the letters because I refused to fire the youth minister. You remember that, don’t you, Kevin? She was angry at the youth minister for kicking her daughter out of the Christmas pageant. It seems the youth minister did not allow sixteen-year-olds to show up intoxicated for rehearsal. Rather than focus on her daughter’s misconduct, Mrs. Satane walked into my office and demanded I fire the youth minister. I refused, of course. Then she lectured me on how she was so generous with her weekly donations. When I suggested some of the money could go towards counseling for her daughter, she almost hit me. I listened to her rant for the next twenty minutes about how important she was in this town and how humiliating it was for her to have her daughter face consequences for her actions. I again suggested to her that she focus her attention on her daughter and not seek vengeance against the youth minister for performing her job well. Mrs. Satane stormed out of my office. Two days later you started to receive letters with all these accusations. When I asked Mrs. Satane in front of you if she wrote the letters, did you she say no?"

"She said that was a terrible thing to accuse her of."

"Did she say 'no'?"

"As I recall you asked her at least three times if she sent the letters, and each time she replied that it was a terrible thing to accuse her of."

"So we agree she never denied it?"

“I dropped the investigation after that. What more did you want?” The Bishop was getting more exasperated by the minute.

“To have some support would have been a good start,” I continued, making my point.

“You know how things are today, John. The Church dropped the ball when some priests were accused of child abuse. That is why we are overly cautious now.”

There was no way I was going to let him get away with that.

“Yes, we had a few criminals masquerading as priests. They should have been dealt with quickly and decisively. And who was it who dropped the ball in this diocese when Father Nefario was accused?”

"I didn't know what to do when that happened. I'm a Bishop, not an investigator. This kind of thing caught me flat-footed. And I'm not the only Bishop who did not know how to deal with these kinds of issues."

"So you did nothing while that pervert moved from parish to parish." I tried to remain calm, but my blood boiled at the memory.

"He couldn't stay in the community. He had to go somewhere."

"He should have gone to jail," I said, as emphatically as I could.

"How many times do I have to repeat myself? I made a mistake." The Bishop appeared to be tiring. A better man would have dropped the matter. I was not trying to hurt him but I was trying to make sure he learned from this mistake.

"And we get to read about it at least once a month in the local newspaper. They keep dredging up the same story even though it happened years ago." It was true. The owners of the paper had the most anti-Catholic agenda I had ever seen. Their journalistic integrity took to a back seat to bashing the Church and everyone who was attending Mass.

"I said I was sorry. We have changed how we handle things, you know."

"I hope so. We're here to serve people and bring them to God, not to make apologies for administrative bungling. Kevin, I can't tell you how angry that subject makes me."

"You know," the Bishop said as he adjusted his shirt sleeves and composed himself, "when I meet with other priests they address me as Bishop O'Reilly, or Your Eminence."

"I guess you straightened me out, Kevin."

"Perhaps I should get to why I am here today."

"For once, we are in agreement." I heaved a huge sigh of relief. It did not matter to me how obvious my impatience was to him.

"You have a very large house here," the Bishop said, as he looked around.

"I have tried selling it and moving to a smaller place. You know that. The market in a town this size just is not conducive to getting a fair price. Especially when so many businesses have closed due to the rough economy."

The Bishop ignored me and continued looking around. He was obviously uncomfortable about what he was going to say.

"Your parish has shrunken in size."

"Yes, the population of the city has gotten smaller. All the churches here have gotten smaller. Some significantly so. A lot of our members were farmers. The farm families get smaller every year as more kids move to Minneapolis."

"Mrs. Satane told me she offered to head up a project to expand the church."

I placed my head in my hands. The nightmare kept getting worse.

"Mrs. Satane contacted you again?"

"Well, yes. She said she would head up a capital project to expand the church. Add more pews in the main church and build some additional meeting rooms."

"And making the church bigger when the number of parishioners are getting fewer – that makes sense to you?" I said incredulously.

“Well, it was a thought.”

“So if we increase the size of the church, it will magically convince people to move to this city?”

The Bishop, incredibly, appeared not to have realized the ridiculousness of what he was saying – until then.

“Perhaps that would be a waste of time.” The Bishop’s understatement was remarkable.

“No, the time wasted does not matter to me. What matters is the fact that Mrs. Satane would tell people to dip into their meager savings and retirement plans to fund this monument to herself. That’s what it would be, wouldn’t it, Kevin?”

The Bishop scratched his chin. “Let’s move on.”

We sat there and stared at each other for a minute. I was desperate to find out what secret he was keeping from me. It was time to prime the pump a little more.

"You're not planning on closing us, are you? We are the only Catholic Church for twenty-five miles. We still make our budget through weekly collections."

"No, certainly not. It is just that money is so tight these days that we need to bring in more. Anything more."

I realized what he was saying was true. And I knew it wasn't my fault.

"Right, the settlement the Diocese paid to the victims of Father Nefario. That really broke the bank, didn't it? I can't say I blame them for suing."

The Bishop was noticeably angered by my bringing that matter up once more.

"Enough, John, enough. Yes, I made a mistake and yet others have to pay for my failures as an administrator. I screwed up. Are we done with that now?"

This time I had triggered a nerve so deep even I felt bad about revisiting the issue. I let it go.

"Go on then."

"In order to keep the diocese running we need more contributions from each parish. That means everyone has to do something extra." He was talking quickly now. "We have the schools to run, the homeless shelter, the food bank, and let's not forget the retirement fund. This diocese has been blessed with dozens of priests who have devoted their entire lives to serving God. We need to take care of them in their golden years."

The Bishop was making sense and being straight. I nodded and gave him my full attention. This encouraged him to continue.

"After thought and deliberation I realized, given the declining numbers in your parish and how well you managed costs, that there was little you could do to help. Then I remembered about the extra rooms you have here."

"How will the rooms help the Diocese?"

"We are going to rent one of your rooms. We used to need all those rooms when this was a young, growing parish but now those spaces sit empty."

The impact of what he was saying really made me angry.

"So we're going to become a rooming house? And my mother will be the maid?" It was bad enough Mom had to still clean up after her middle-aged son. I did not want her doing the same for a stranger.

"No, no. He will be responsible for his own meals. Evie will not have to do anything extra."

"I'll hold you to that. Now, who are you moving in? Are we talking about a man of the cloth here? I suppose it is one of those retired priests you mentioned."

The Bishop had a funny look on his face as he nodded yes.

"A man of the cloth, yes. Absolutely. He is."

"Why do you keep affirming my question?

"He is a man of the cloth." I wondered how many times he was going to repeat that.

“Got that. And I feel there’s a little bit more?”

“His name is Carl Carter. He is not retired.”

“Hmmm,” I puzzled. “I thought I knew every priest in this diocese. The name doesn’t ring a bell. Is he from out of state? A retiree from somewhere else?”

“He is a Protestant. A Lutheran minister. Reverend Carl Carter.”

I sat silently, pondering the many ways my small world was being shattered.

“You are speechless? God has answered my prayers,” the Bishop joked. I think he was joking.

“A Protestant? Living with a Catholic priest? I should check my calendar. It’s not April Fool’s Day, is it?”

"It is a wonderful opportunity to show the community that we all serve the same God and get along, regardless of how we do so." I so hated it when the Bishop made sense.

"And we make some money while we're at it." I made a fist salute.

"And Carl has a place to live."

"Carl? So you two are on a first name basis. Sounds like you're great chums. How do you refer to me when you're talking with others?"

"John . . ." the Bishop bit his lip.

"That's okay," I reassured him, "sometimes ignorance is bliss."

"It is indeed funny how things work out. Perhaps it was Divine Providence. I was at a conference of Christian church leaders last month. I sat down with one of the leaders of the Lutheran Synod, Reverend Melcher."

The Bishop was starting to ramble, telling me things I did not need or want to know. There was a need for a lot more details. I started to nod my heads sideways to give him a nonverbal cue to get back on track. It did not work.

"Yes, and we got to talking. He told me about the financial problems they are having. It seems they are in similar straits here."

"Here? You mean in the city of Blessing?"

"Yes. The Reverend is committed to keeping the church open. The only way they can do so is to cut costs. Unlike us they had a newer house where the Reverend lived and had no problems selling it. The money from the sale, along with no more maintenance costs, means they will be able to keep their church open. They can pay a reasonable amount of rent for the Reverend and still be money ahead. Everyone wins."

I had had a moment to compose my thoughts while the Bishop continued discussing how this idea came about. I was starting to feel outrage at how this process was conducted. The Bishop's idea, though good, maybe even great, should have been discussed with me first.

"You know, Kevin, I am very unhappy about this. You absolutely should have come to me with this idea before you rented out a room in my house. I'm not saying it is a bad idea; I am talking about the way you did it."

"It is not your house, it belongs to the Diocese. Nothing is expected of Evie. The Reverend can cook and clean for himself." I knew the Bishop was right. I had sinned by claiming the house was mine. It was not mine, and I knew better. He had covered my main concern about Mom.

A better man would have kept quiet.

“Kevin, you are correct that it is not my house, but it is my home. And my mother’s. Don’t you think that out of respect you could have talked with me first?”

“It all happened very fast. I apologize for the surprise. But the decision is made.”

I was still upset with this and more than willing to stir the pot.

“Well, gee, Kevin. What happens if I like this guy so much I convert and leave the priesthood?”

“I will throw a party.” The Bishop felt good about that one-liner. He should have. It was a good one.

"Can't say as I would blame you." This honest statement elicited a wide grin from the Bishop.

"Well then, Your Eminence, what happens if we get into a real heavyweight theological debate and really get at each other's throats?

"Are you not capable of a heavyweight theological debate?" he asked.

"Good point. But we will live in the same house. What happens if we don't get along?"

"You *will* live together – as BROTHERS – as an example of how God's people do not just tolerate but love each other." Now the Bishop was using his forceful voice. He was serious. Me, less so.

"Living together as brothers? Sounds Biblical, Kevin."

“Yes, now I am liking what you are saying.” He seemed pleased to hear this.

“Biblical brothers. Like Cain and Abel. You’re hoping for us to turn out like them? Which one of us did you want murdered? See, I did go to the Seminary. I just don’t like using that theological stuff unless it’s absolutely necessary.”

“My liking for what you were saying did not last long. To answer your next question, John, no, I am not surprised.”

The reality is there wasn’t much for me to complain about. He was the boss. The decision was his to make. It was time to move on. Besides, I had tormented the poor man enough. I sat quietly and folded my hands.

My silence told the Bishop he had won this round.

“So, when does the Reverend Carl move in? I raised a white flag, but it was a truce, not a surrender.

A look of intense relief came over the Bishop’s face. I suspect his blood pressure dropped, too. At least now I did not have to worry about him having a stroke in my living room.

We spent the rest of the meeting discussing the new left-handed pitcher playing for Minnesota. When the subject was theology, I respected the Bishop’s insight and knowledge more than anyone I knew. When it came to baseball I could not say the same.

CHAPTER TWO

Mom was ecstatic at the thought of someone new moving in. Always much more social than myself, she needed more people in her life. The life of a priest's mother was not easy. She had friends, but I expect they always wondered if she was reporting back to me about their lives and actions. Of course, I knew she was not the kind of person who would betray a friend's confidence. But people, especially those who are conscious of their sins, tend to worry.

At first when I told her about my conversation with the Bishop, she thought another priest was moving in. Her faith was far stronger than mine and I understood she would relish the chance to talk with another priest about what God meant to her. My being her son meant our conversations were always a little different from how she would discuss matters with another priest.

When I told her we would be hosting a Lutheran minister she, being mom, perked right up and thought it would be exciting. She said it would provide more "depth" to our faith, or some such wording like that.

Mom was never one to take my side no matter how right I was . . . okay, in this case I was wrong. It made sense and I knew it. The idea would result in an easy, steady revenue stream for the diocese. And even better we would be setting an example of cooperation between the Catholic and Lutheran churches. We would be showing the city that the commonality in our beliefs outweighed the differences. Genius of an idea, really. All of it spoiled by the fact that the credit went to my nemesis the Bishop. Oh, well.

The few days before the invader arrived went peacefully. I did not, and would not, make any plans to adjust my schedule or activities.

The afternoon of the event I sat in my easy chair watching Minnesota lose a baseball game. It was not one of their better games, but it took my mind off my woes.

"Johnny," Mom excitedly asked, "shouldn't you be getting ready for Reverend Carl? He should be here any minute now."

"Getting ready? What is there to do?"

"Well, I don't know. I have lunch ready. I hope he likes Irish stew."

"You do remember, Mom, that he is responsible for his own meals."

"Yes, of course. But since he will be living here as part of our family, I thought it would be a great way to make him feel welcome."

“Family? Part of *our* family?” I gave her my sternest look.

“Practice what we preach?” Her voice was politely reminding me I needed to step up to the plate. Why couldn’t God have given me a less intelligent mother? Someone who wasn’t a much better person than myself? Oh, the burdens of this earthly life.

Mom stood by me as I pretended to be watching the game. She that “mother” look on her face, pretending to look displeased while fighting a smile.

“Anything else you want to tell me, Johnny?”

“I have, fortunately, no idea what you are talking about.”

“I went into Carl’s room one last time to make sure everything was in order.”

"You didn't have to do that. Cleaning is his responsibility." I was caught by my mother. Things never change no matter how old you get. The only mature thing to do was feign innocence.

"I found that large statue of the Virgin Mary. You know, the one that used to sit in the garden. Someone cleaned it up and carried it upstairs. Would you please move it back into the garden? Or you could put it in my room."

"Oh, right." Not a clever reply, but it used to work when she reprimanded me for stealing cookies.

"And you, as a priest, know that Lutherans don't have the same devotion to Mary we Catholics do, right?"

"Now that you mention it . . ." I couldn't wait for this conversation to be over.

I looked at my wristwatch and then at the wall clock.

"Where is that Carl? I thought timeliness was supposed to be a Protestant virtue."

"You can always drive to Mankato if you feel the need to go to confession, dear. Father Hanson has such a gift for reconciling sinners." Mom was really putting me in my place.

"Maybe I'll go to the good Reverend Carl. Oh, wait. Those people don't do that kind of thing, do they?"

"Maybe he does not need to." Mom smiled. She won. She always won. And I loved her for it.

I was aware, during our conversation, of a car pulling into the drive. I waited until the inevitable knock on the door. I slowly got up and walked to the door. With a shrug of resignation I opened it to see a man, my age and my size, with a look of anxiety that no doubt mirrored my own.

"John? My name is Carl. Carl Carter."

"Yes, I am *Father* John. Good to meet you, Carl." I extended my hand all the while realizing what a horses' rear end I had come across as.

"Um, *Father* John. Is that how you would like me to address you?"

"Oh, well, everyone calls me Father. It's just a habit."

"Right, I understand. Since I'm not Catholic, that's a bit awkward," said Carl, reluctantly but clearly. "Call me Carl."

"Well, anyway, okay," I muttered. "Carl. I like that name. Yes, quite fine."

Mom was allowing me a minute to make a good impression. Since I had tragically failed, she took it upon herself to pick up the slack.

“You must be the Reverend Carl. Welcome,” Mom gushed. She was genuine in her friendliness. I wondered sometimes if I was adopted.

“Thank you. You may call me Carl. Everyone does.”

“And please, call me Evie. Everyone calls me that except for John.”

Carl smiled. “John? Oh, you mean *Father*.”

The Reverend looked slyly over at me. Somehow providence had placed two wise guys in the same house. My penance would be stiff and daily.

Mom, of course, had to speak up. “Goodness, don’t call him *Father*. You live here. You’re family now. Call him *John*.”

Carl smiled. The realization that it was two against one made me grimace.

“Okay, then,” Carl said with a shrug. “John, it is.”

Mom, once she got started, couldn’t stop. “Well, I’ll leave you two to get acquainted. Please, Carl, sit down.”

Mom left the room. Carl and I sat across from each other. Silence ruled the room.

Two minutes that felt like three weeks dragged by. After an eternity Mom came back in the room. She seemed to be able to sense that neither of us had spoken a word during her absence. I think she felt she had to say something, so she blurted out, “Carl, I have your room all set up for you now. I hope you two have been having a nice chat."

"Well, at least we haven't been disagreeing about anything," I honestly replied.

"If you'll excuse me," Carl delicately said, "I need to spend some time in my room working on my sermon."

I picked up the remote control and turned the game back on.

Mom, being the sweet person she was, had to go the extra mile. "Don't be a stranger. We expect you down here to watch the baseball game with us. I trust you're a Minnesota fan."

"Ah, actually, I'm a New York fan."

Mom was firmly back in my camp. We both glared at the good Reverend. He slowly walked away.

CHAPTER THREE

The next day arrived. I stretched out in bed, secure in the fact that everything that happened the day before was simply a bad dream.

It was life back to normal. Apparently Carl was a late riser. I had a peaceful breakfast while Mom read the newspaper. My greatest fear, that I would have to face Carl first thing every morning, was a lot of worry over nothing.

After morning Mass I came back to the house for breakfast. I studied my schedule while Mom did some housework. There were a number of parishioners on my schedule today. Next to saying Mass, counseling my flock was the highlight of my daily life. Bringing comfort while helping people find Jesus in their lives was a great treasure that I embraced with all my heart. Every day in my life was another confirmation that I was the luckiest man in the world to be a parish priest.

My first appointment was with Mrs. Smith. A kind, decent woman who was perpetually nervous, Mrs. Smith was always concerned with hell and her inevitable place in it. The good people worried about hell. The people who were speeding their way to perdition on a non-stop speeding locomotive never seemed to be give the afterlife a second thought.

I heard a car pull up.

"Mom, it is Mrs. Smith. We have a short appointment this morning. I'll take her into my office."

Just then there was a knock on the door. I couldn't figure out how Mrs. Smith had got from her car to the door so quickly. The look of surprise on my face when I opened the door must have been amusing.

“Carl?” I asked, as my mind tried to understand what was going on.

“Sorry to bother you, John.” Carl was wiping his face with a towel as he stood on the front step. ”I like to run a few miles every morning. I am so used to leaving my door unlocked that I forgot to bring my key with me. Don’t worry, it won’t happen again.”

“Oh, ah, no problem, Carl.” It was then that I noticed Mrs. Smith had arrived on the front step and was standing right behind my athletic housemate. Now it was Carl’s turn to be surprised. He turned and smiled at her.

“Well,” I stammered as I tried to regain my composure, “Mrs. Smith, please come in.”

Realizing that I had to introduce the two of them, I reluctantly made the grand announcement.

"Mrs. Smith, this is Carl." I glanced over at the interloper. He was visibly upset at what he viewed as a slight. "Excuse me. The Reverend Carl Carver. He is a Lutheran minister."

Mrs. Smith looked over at Carl and you could see the light bulb come on over her head.

"Oh, I know who you are. One of my sewing circle friends goes to your church. She speaks very highly of you." Mrs. Smith looked back at me knowingly and said the words that pierced my soul. "So you two are friends."

Now I was the one who was visibly upset. There was no way to deal with this. I could have taken the high road but I decided the cowardly way worked best for me.

"Mrs. Smith, we should leave the good Reverend alone and have our meeting." With that, I started walking through the hallway to my office. I quickly realized that I was all alone.

“Oh, there is no hurry,” Mrs. Smith politely stated. “It is so nice to have two men of the cloth here.”

“But only one Catholic,” I reminded her.

“Do you know what my mother used to say to me when I was a little girl?” Mrs. Smith asked.

I did not know what her mother used to tell her. I could gladly have lived the rest of my life blissfully ignorant.

“Two heads are better than one! That is what she used to tell me. Maybe both of you should sit down with me.” Mrs. Smith was delighted with herself for coming up with this idea.

Suicide was against my religion. So was homicide. That left me with few options.

“Well, let’s move into my office, then,” I surrendered.

The only thing that could have made it worse was what happened next. Mom came out of my office just as we got to the door.

“I have your office dusted, Johnny.” She then saw Mrs. Smith and corrected herself. “Father.”

“That’s great. Thank you. Please excuse us.”

“Oh, Evie! How nice to see you,” Mrs. Smith gushed. I wondered if she wanted my mother to attend the meeting also. Maybe we could find a stray cat as well.

“I am sorry, but we need to keep on our schedule.” I pushed things along. The sooner we got this over with the quicker I could sit alone and wallow in self-pity.

“Schedule?” Mom queried, helpful as always. Next she would remind me I had no other appointments and could spend the entire morning working with this Martin Luther want-to-be.

I guided Mrs. Smith and the Reverend busybody into my office. Mrs. Smith took the chair in front of my desk and unfortunately there was an extra chair for Carl too.

Each year I gave a homily on taking up a challenge during a difficult time. This would be such a time and it was important that I did what I asked my parishioners to do. It would also be a great opportunity to show Carl how a priest worked. Here was one of my parishioners in what I assumed was a tough spiritual place. Who knew what difficult path she was treading today? As her spiritual leader I would provide her with a compassionate ear, guidance and direction that would lead her out of her present difficulty and someday result in heaven. I could wait no longer for this chance to show Carl the complexity of the issues I dealt with on a daily basis. Gently, I asked Mrs. Smith to share why she was here today.

"I am going to hell," she whimpered.

Pure speculation on my part, of course, but I was convinced this woman had never done anything bad in her life, save for her never-ending feelings of guilt.

"Please, Mrs. Smith. Tell me more," I said.

"It's my muppy boy," Mrs. Smith sadly stated in response to my query.

I glanced over at Carl. He was as confused as I was. That was reassuring; it meant I didn't mis-hear.

"Muppy boy?" I asked, hoping it would quickly make sense.

Mrs. Smith nodded. Tears started coming to her eyes.

"Muppy. My little darling. My sweet little boy."

"Mrs. Smith, I know your boys. Neither of them is named Muppy. They are both adults."

"Yes, and thanks to your guidance they became the fine young men they are today."

I desperately wanted to change the subject because I knew what was coming and I didn't need Carl to hear it.

"Why, both of them come up for parole next year." Mrs. Smith was pleased at the thought of these two fine upstanding car thieves being released back into society.

I copped another glance at Carl. He was fighting a smirk. The smirk was winning the battle.

"Again, Mrs. Smith," I reluctantly prompted her to continue. "Can you tell me, er, us, who muppy boy is?"

"My terrier. My doggy."

"Muppy is a dog? Your dog?" I confirmed.

"Yes, and after what happened this morning I am afraid I am going to hell."

After a few seconds of hesitation I pumped the well some more.

"What happened this morning?"

"Muppy did his business on the carpet. His dirty little business. And I just had the carpet cleaned. Professionally cleaned. I was so upset I slapped his little behind."

Mrs. Smith stared at me, tears flowing down her cheeks. I was fairly well established in theology but not so good in dog psychology.

"And then what?" I questioned.

Mrs. Smith looked at me quizzically. She shook her head at the thought that I did not understand.

"I spanked my little boy. And he yelped. How could I be so cruel?" The tears kept coming.

"So," I took a deep breath, "you spanked your dog for wetting the carpet. And you are concerned that act will send you to hell."

The woman-ogre shook her head in an affirmative manner.

I looked around the room as I tried to compose a response. Accidentally, I made eye contact Carl. He seemed less amused that he did at first. It occurred to me that he was as unsure as I was as to how to handle this. Many people, including this woman, consider their dogs to be more than family. Their pets are all they have in their lives. As ridiculous as this seemed on the surface, the woman could be crushed by not taking her situation seriously.

"Mrs. Smith," I began, "you love Muppy as you love your sons, don't you?"

"Yes, I do," she responded.

"And you spanked your sons while they were growing up, didn't you?" I guessed the answer was yes.

"Oh, no. I never spanked them. I thought it would crush their spirits." My guess was wrong. But this was beginning to make sense.

“Okay then. And you don’t want Muppy to wind up in trouble, like your sons did?”

“Oh no! I couldn’t take that. I need to see Muppy every day.”

“Okay. Then I think Muppy will remember the punishment you gave him. And he will try to stay out of trouble. That is the point of spanking.”

“I never knew that.”

“MMM hmmmm.” I said this as I looked over at Carl. He was rolling his eyes.

“The very fact that you spanked Muppy to keep him out of trouble, not to be cruel to him, means that you will not be heading to hell.”

Mrs. Smith jumped up from her chair and clasped her hands together as if praying.

"Oh, thank you, Father! I feel such a burden lifted from my shoulders. I am going to go home now and tell my husband. And I will tell him spanking is okay. As long as you are certain it is okay for both of us to spank?"

My tiredness with the issue had gotten the best of me. "We're still talking about the dog?"

"The dog, my dog, my Muppy boy. Yes." Mrs. Smith either did not catch on or chose not to show it.

I heard a muffled noise coming from Carl. His hand was over his mouth. Apparently the man had a sense of humor. I guess I caught him a bit by surprise.

I rose from my chair and walked to the door. I opened it and motioned my hand through it.

"Mrs. Smith, I hope this time was helpful to you."

"Father, it's so great to have you to turn to when my soul is troubled. Thank you for listening to my confession. I was certain I was going to hell.

I took her arm and gently helped her out the door. "Yes, well, that's all good and fine. Good day to you."

Mrs. Smith walked towards the front door and then paused. I considered this to be a bad sign.

"Oh, Father. I almost forgot I brought you a bag of homemade cookies. Here you go," she said, as she handed me a large sack. I thanked her profusely and escorted her to the door. I watched her walk to the door as Mom reappeared from wherever she had been hiding. She watched as I put the sack in the garbage.

"Aren't you going to eat the cookies, Johnny?"

"I'm a priest, not a saint."

"Her cookies chipped your teeth the last time you tried to eat them, didn't they?"

"Yes, mom. Remember we gave the rest of the cookies to the dog?"

"Oh, Johnny, he had such a belly ache. It lasted all night."

I walked into the living room and turned on the television. The meeting with Mrs. Smith was so short I had ample time before my next appointment. My recliner was begging for some me time and I gave in. But Mom was not done with me yet. She hovered next to me as I picked up the remote control and started channel surfing.

"Johnny, is this what you are going to do the rest of the day?"

I rolled my eyes. She always hated when I did that as a kid. My hope was that it would work better now than it did then, at getting her to give me a break. No such luck.

"I just don't think a man of the cloth . . ." Mom had a way of saying this and then letting her voice drift off that was really effective and bugging me. It was, however, ineffective at getting me to do what she wanted. She knew this. After fifty years you would think she would change. I knew where my stubbornness came from. I turned up the volume on the television.

Mom walked over and grabbed the remote control. She turned off the television.

“Dear, do you remember the discussion we had a few days about that important commandment?”

“I still haven’t killed anyone.” I reached for the remote and mom pulled it away from me. “Though the temptation is sometimes strong.”

“Now, Johnny. If priests don’t respect their mothers, how can you expect anyone else to do so?”

“I think there is a commandment about letting your son watch highlights from last night’s baseball game.”

“You always did have a sense of humor. It has always made me smile.”

“It is just one of the many things about me that you love.”

"Okay, find something on television that is more important than the souls of your congregation. Enjoy yourself."

"I am the priest here. I am the only who should be making people feel guilty, not you."

"They won't let women be priests. And a good thing, too, because if I was a priest you never would have been born."

"So far today, I have said Mass, handled parish office duties, listened to a woman who is as of free of sin as any saint confess to housebreaking her dog, and I just want a few minutes to myself."

"Maybe you should take advantage of your situation and not spend so much time alone."

"Alone? I am never alone, Mom. Did you forget you live here?"

"I meant Reverend Carter."

"Carl," I corrected her. The one thing I was not about to tolerate was him being referred to as a reverend.

"Where is he? Where did he go after talking with Mrs. Smith?"

"I don't know. Maybe he went to his room to pray or whatever those Lutherans do when no one is watching."

"You could ask him to watch your baseball game with you. That would make him feel welcome, don't you think?"

Years of priestly duties had given me the ability to stare down anyone. Anyone but my mother. I tried anyway. It didn't work.

"I hardly think that is a Christian attitude."

"What would you like me to do – go up and pray with him? I'd gladly kneel down with him but I don't think *those people* do that kind of thing."

"John, if he's going to be living here you should at least try to get along. Why don't you do an activity together?"

Now I had to stop what little I was doing and find an institution where mom could happily live the rest of her life.

"An activity? Maybe we could discuss Martin Luther's singing voice."

"I don't know what you should do, but do something. You're driving me crazy moping around like this. I have not seen you this depressed since you were fifteen and you and Jenny Lynn broke up."

Great, now our conversation had turned to discussing an old girlfriend. What priest does not enjoy doing that? Well, if I could not agitate mom with this subject, I would really be losing my touch.

"She was beautiful, wasn't she?" I had firmly baited the hook.

"Watch your thoughts, *FATHER*." Now she seemed upset.

"It's not like I'm going to rush out and ask her to marry me. It's been more than thirty years and my current status is and shall remain "single." I am firmly head over heels in love with my church." I paused a minute while I drew a breath. "My vocation is the best thing that could ever happen to me. Thanks to God for showing me how I could best serve Him. I find such joy in serving God." Somehow my plan to agitate Mom went astray. There was just so much happiness in the priesthood that it even eclipsed my daily battle with my mother.

"You have found your calling, Johnny. Your sacrifices have meaning."

Just then Carl walked in. I looked over at him. I could not help saying what I said.

"Speaking of sacrifices," I muttered.

Carl either did not hear me or chose to ignore me. He seemed to have a talent for the latter.

"Hi, folks. Mind if I join you?"

"This is your home now, Carl, please come and do whatever you want. We want to know how everything is going for you. Is your room okay?" Mom was concerned and compassionate. She really wanted him to feel at home. I loved her in spite of her lack of flaws.

"Very nice." Carl paused a minute, trying to think of how to put his next statement. "The statue of the Virgin Mary is very nice, too. I have never seen one that big inside a house before. Is that . . . common in Catholic households?"

"I trust you were able to manage regardless of the distraction of our Lord's mother. The mother of Jesus, our Savior. It is my fault for burdening you the image of our holy mother." I was clumsy but made up for it with a certain heavy handedness.

I decided to finish with a flourish.

"I hope it doesn't offend you. I went to a lot of work to carry that up there."

"Johnny," mom said, "I think you were going to move that statue, weren't you, dear?"

"Of course. I would not want our guest to be upset," I quipped.

Carl, bless his Protestant heart, decided to take up the challenge.

“Well, I did not pay much attention to the statue. I was busy reading the Bible. Nothing like reading the Bible to fortify myself in times of stress. You Catholics . . . you do, on occasion, read the Bible, don’t you?” Carl placed his pauses carefully as he pleasantly took up his part in the duel.

“Bible,” I said quizzically, “big, black book? I think there’s a copy around here somewhere. Oh, yes. We put it under the leg of that plant stand to keep it from falling over.”

“John, I am glad God has put us together in the same home. I imagine we’ll have some great theological discussions, you and I.”

“You mean debates.”

“Friendly debates?” Carl was extending an olive branch. To me, olives were only useful when used in martinis.

“Maybe I should have said arguments.”

“Well, John, we both believe in the same God, do we not?” He was trying, but I was not ready to accept surrender. “It is interesting how much our faiths have in common.”

“Ever been to Vatican City?” I asked.

“I’ve heard of it. It’s in Italy, isn’t it? Doesn’t someone famous live there? A guy who wears a big hat?”

“It is where our spiritual leader lives. You know, the leader of all Christians.” We needed to start off on the right foot. To my way of thinking the right foot meant not an acknowledgment but more importantly an acceptance of my beliefs.

"You Catholics do not know there is more than one way to heaven, don't you? Perhaps a better way."

"Well, this should get me a quick pass through purgatory," I mused.

"Purgatory?" Carl smiled. "That's something those in my faith don't worry about."

"One more minute with you and I won't need to worry, either." I took comfort where I could find it.

"Maybe we should change the subject, John?" I sensed Carl weakening. Or maybe turning the other cheek. I hated it when people took Jesus's advice.

"So right, Carl. No reason to think the two of us would have anything to say about religion. I find playing a game is a good way to get to know someone. Do you play any games?"

"I thought we were playing one now," Carl remarked innocently.

Mom let out her best "Mom" sigh.

"All these years I wished I had given you a brother. Now I know God was truly blessing me by giving me girls after you were born."

"Boys do play differently, Evie," Carl assured her.

Mom went over to the living room cabinet and got out the chess board. She placed it on the table between the two recliners. "Maybe you two could do some productive with your time." She turned and left.

I let out as heavy a sigh as I could. Carl's face was nondescript. I began to think he could be a poker player at least in virtue.

I began to set up the game. There was no point in asking him if he wanted to play. Mom committed to us to the game as if we were misbehaving five-year-old children. I explained the rules as quickly as I could. Nothing is more frustrating than having to explain a game to someone. There is always such a learning curve. I mused to myself that someday maybe Carl would learn enough to win a game here and there.

We began playing. Carl was a quick study. I told him the first moves to make and after that he seemed to catch on quickly. Too quickly. Luck would not explain some of the moves he made.

His luck ran out. Carl made a basic, horrible mistake. I had never seen anyone expose their queen so openly at this stage of the game. I swallowed hard and tried to restrain myself so I wouldn't make him feel bad.

"Carl, that's a real dangerous place to move your queen," I corrected him.

“Should I return it to where it was?” he wondered.

“No, no. The way the game is played, once you move a piece, it is moved.”

“Fair enough. You did tell me that.”

Desperate to be decent about this, I decided to explain what was about to happen.

“You see, I am going to move my rook here. And then in two more moves I will checkmate you.”

“Hmmmm” was the only sound Carl could get past his lips.

I studied his face. One does not perform the duties of a priest without being able to read faces. Carl did have a tremendous poker face but I was slowly peeling the layers off.

“GOOD LORD!” my mind shouted to myself as I saw through the façade Carl was presenting. He was trying to hide a sense of glee. Carl had a trick up his sleeve and was, to his credit, not gloating about it. I realized that while I had been trying to educate him in this game, he had been plotting his moves. I put my hand over my face as I realized what was about to happen.

“I think then, I’ll move my queen here,” Carl modestly stated. He then looked down at his feet.

“A wonderful move!” I congratulated him on his checkmate. “Incredible beginner’s luck.” I thought my playing the innocent would siphon the truth out.

Carl blushed a little. He knew he would have to come clean. “I played a little bit in college,” he confessed.

“A little bit?” I gave the priestly smile I used when convincing someone they should tell me all their sins, not just a few.

“Well, my team won the state championship. I was the captain.”

“I think they picked the right fellow,” I had to admit.

Carl seemed quite relieved that I was gracious. And why shouldn’t I be? A first class sneak appreciates another first class sneak whenever he meets him. Carl was quiet, which meant it was taking longer to size him up than most people. A big mouthed person who cannot stop talking, usually about themselves, is no challenge to understand. All people like that care about is themselves. Carl was well suited for his position. His personality blended well with the needs of a man of the cloth. Except for the sneakiness. Maybe especially because of the sneakiness.

“I am going up to my room for a while to pray,” I calmly stated.

Carl, innocently enough, asked, "Any special intentions I can pray along with you?"

"I don't think so. I need to pray for forgiveness for harboring bad thoughts." With that I gave Carl a knowing look and proceeded to my room. Half the fun would be imagining his thoughts. Perhaps he would feel a bit guilty about taking advantage of my good nature. Perhaps he would be worried about whether I would kick him out of my house. Either way, it was a win-win situation.

Mom and Carl had a good get-to-know-you conversation during which she educated him about who was really running the show in this house.

"Carl, how did the chess game go?" Mom looked him right in the eye when she said it.

"It was okay, Evie." A less innocent statement was never made.

"Did you win?" The guilt trip began.

"It was very close, Evie."

"I did not ask you if it was close, Carl." Mom firmly pulled him back to the fear only a fifteen old knew when faced with an angry parent.

"Yes, I did win," Carl admitted as he stared at his feet.

"But you did tell Johnny that you were a chess champion before you began playing, didn't you?"

"Well, he knows that. Now he knows that. He kind of figured things out."

"Figuring things out is one of his specialties."

"It sounds like it runs in the family. How did you know I was a chess champion?"

"Did you think I would allow someone into my house without checking them out? Unlike my son I, am very comfortable searching the internet."

"No, ma'am. I guess not." Carl's line of vision slowly rose to meet Mom's. A slight smile came to his face. The feeling that same fifteen year old felt when he no longer feared the parent, but came to respect and admire her. "Your house? I thought the Archdiocese owned the house."

"Someone is looking to be sent to bed without dessert." Mom crossed her arms.

"Evie, I think I am really going to enjoy living here."

“We’ll see about that.” Mom turned and walked away. She had accepted this stranger into not just the house, but her family. Now I was truly abandoned.

CHAPTER FOUR

A partly cloudy, cool day with a slight breeze meant we were content to spend some time indoors.

The three of us – that is correct, sadly – the three of us sat watching television. To be exact, we were watching baseball. I was in such a wonderful mood. My mood was not affected by Mom's continued dirty looks.

"Another hitless inning for the hapless NEEEEWWWW Yorkers. We are really teaching them how to play baseball tonight!" I exclaimed. Rubbing it in felt so good, so very good. I was going to be spending a lot of time in confession the next time I went to visit my friend, Fr. Stanislaus.

Carl winced a bit then offered, "I hope you'll be half this happy at the Second Coming of Jesus."

“Until that happens, this will do just fine.”

Mom could only take so much from her two boys, one hers by birth, the other adopted a bit late in life. “You two should be ashamed. Years ago I was disappointed God didn’t answer my prayers and give me another little boy in my family. Now fifty years later, I appreciate that he gave me a half century of peace.”

“You were an only child?” Carl’s knowledge of our family was limited up to now.

“Only boy. I have two sisters. They both live in Wisconsin.” I could see what Carl was thinking. “No, I don’t think they moved there to get away from me. Mom gets over to visit them a few times year. It’s a double vacation for her to spend some time with them and away from me.”

"Oh, Johnny," Mom said. "Now you are being silly. I love to see my girls and my grandchildren. And Wisconsin is so beautiful. Every time I go there I understand why they love it so much."

"Green Bay Packer fans?" Carl asked, to my disbelief. Why would he ask such a thing?

"We love them anyway," Mom interjected.

"As if we care what sports team they cheer for." I attempted to show the unimportance of this topic of discussion.

"Well, actually, we pray for their conversion." Mom said this, and now it was I who prayed that Carl would take it as a joke.

"Yes, prayers for conversion. Maybe we should add you, Carl, to the list."

Carl looked at me with bewilderment. He did not know if I was serious. “Conversion for sports teams or religion?” For the first time since I met him, he was serious.

“Johnny, someday your humor is going to get you in trouble.” Mom again tried to calm the storm.

The desire to stir the pot was taking hold of my better judgment.

“And you, Carl. What football team do you cheer for?”

Always quick on the draw, mom returned to the original subject. “My oldest daughter, Shelley, she’s been married now for twenty-five years. My Junie has been married for almost twenty years.”

Carl must have decided to save his energy for a battle on another day. He followed mom’s lead.

“Wonderful! Grandkids?”

"Yes, four of them. I love spending time with them. I'd go more often, but I'm needed here."

I had several snappy comebacks. As I was deciding which one to spew forth, I was caught up in mom's glaring eyes. She put her hands on her hips. That was usually one step away from real trouble.

God's great mercy shone forth in a small miracle. The telephone rang.

Mom answered the phone. "Yes, Mrs. Harvey. Father John is here. No, he is not busy. It sounds like you need to speak with Father. We'll be expecting you."

Mom put the phone down and turned to leave the room. "Mrs. Harvey will be here in fifteen minutes."

"Did she say what it was about?"

"Forgive me, Carl, for asking this. I don't mean to be rude. Johnny, may we talk about this or is it confidential?"

"I can leave the room. There is no offense taken."

"Wait," I stopped Carl from getting up his chair, "he is a man of the cloth, same as me. It is not unusual to get consultation from a peer." A few days ago, I could not think of calling him a peer. Honestly, I am not creative or smart enough to come up with the wording I did. The Holy Spirit must have been moving deep within me.

"She had another argument with Joe," Mom explained. "That's all she said over the phone."

"That's her husband," I told Carl.

“Hmmm. Is this a recurring issue?” Carl asked.

“This is not unusual, they fight all the time.” I tried to bring Carl up to speed.

“I am a certified Marriage Counselor. If there is anything I can do . . .”

“I also am a marriage counselor,” I said, to set matters straight.

Mom tried to explain further. “It’s complicated. Mixed marriage.”

“Oh, I see. In today’s modern society it’s not that big of a deal if a white person and a person of color marry.”

“That’s not it, Carl.”

“*Mixed marriage* – she’s Catholic and he’s Lutheran.” Mom further explained.

“Tsk, tsk. There should be a law against that, don’t you think?” Carl had a sense of humor. It was weird but something clicked in my head when he said that. The Holy Spirit had shaken some creativity into my brain.

“Mom, can you get on the phone quickly? Call Mrs. Harvey back.” I was concerned that Mrs. Harvey was already out the door.

“I can try. Why?”

“Ask her to bring her husband. Is that okay with you Carl – if he talks to you while I am meeting with her? Otherwise, he’ll just stay home and sulk. Maybe this will help.”

“I like to feel useful when I can. Of course.”

Mom dialed the phone. “Sue? Bring Joe. I know he doesn’t want to meet with a priest. We have a Lutheran minister here. What?

It's a long story. Joe can talk with Carl, the Reverend Carl, while you talk with Father John."

Mom put the phone down. She walked over and placed a hand on each of our shoulders.   The look on her face was one of knowing satisfaction.

Each of us forced a smile.

CHAPTER FIVE

It was time to compare notes. Each of us had spent over an hour speaking with our respective clients. Then the four of us got together. That went on for another forty-five minutes. In the group, Carl sat back and let me take the lead. I appreciated that he knew his place and did not try to take over. My entire career I had flown solo. Working in tandem had never occurred to me and I certainly had no training or blessing in such a situation. It was amazing how well it worked, but what really stunned me was how much fun it was.

I felt as if I was going to explode with enthusiasm. "I can't believe how well that worked. It's the first time I've ever seen the Harveys smile at each other."

Carl interrupted, but it was okay. "Joe said he always felt left out when Sue would come up here by herself. Coming here together really made a difference for him."

"Once we got them both calmed down we were able to get them to work together. It is something when two people who should work together don't, for silly reasons."

I realized, with some degree of horror, what I just said. I tried to look calm and pretend I was not embarrassed. After a few seconds I looked over at Carl. He was trying his best to pretend he did not notice anything about what I said. He continued talking, I think, to help me feel like he did not hear me.

"They said they haven't felt this good about themselves in years." Carl smiled and then continued, "If it is okay with you I would like to continue working together with them. They are not out of the woods yet."

I nodded. Carl was playing second fiddle to me. I knew he was used to, as was I, taking the lead. I appreciated his acting with such dignity and class.

Mom walked into the room. She was bursting at the seams. I tried to make eye contact to make sure she did not say anything that would ruin the moment.

She was restrained, much to my relief.

"Everything go okay, boys?" Mom asked.

"Well," I nonchalantly stated, "we wound up missing the baseball game."

"I should slap you." She joked as she crossed her arms. "Well, I have laundry to do. I'll leave you two trouble-makers to get back to your mischief." With that Mom walked away.

"Slap you?" Carl smiled. "Doesn't she have to go to confession for that?"

"Only if she actually did it."

"I had no idea Evie could be violent." Then he looked at me slyly. "Should I be worried?"

"Oh no. Worrying will do you no good. She always waits to kill people until they are sleeping. You won't even know until it's too late."

"Now that you mention it, there is no lock on my door."

"We removed the lock. Mom's hands are old and it was too hard for her to pick them."

"So I'm not the first tenant you've had?"

"Just make sure the rent is paid promptly each month. And maybe you'll be okay.....for a while." Carl nodded.

We sat there a few minutes, growing more uncomfortable each second.

"Been a long night, Carl. I'm heading to bed." I took the coward's way out.

"Me, too. Good night."

I sat on my bed for a long time. Never one to withhold anything from God, I started speaking, in a whisper, these words: "Dear God, I know I am not much of a man and have not served you as well as I should. But tonight I realized my biggest flaw. Flaw? No – my biggest sin. I have not given you thanks for everything you have done for me. I offer my thanks to you for everything you have done. You have always provided me with everything I needed. I have a mother who loves me and takes care of me. I have my true vocation of loving and serving you. And now you have given me the one thing I did not know I was lacking but truly needed. A friend."

I turned off the light and lay back in my bed. Gazing silently at nothing more than the paint on my ceiling, I began to drift off to sleep. As my need for slumber overtook me, I thought I heard Carl through the wall speaking these words:

"Dear God, I have always served you the best I could. When you took my darling Betty to heaven five years ago I tried not to complain. I had no desire to re-marry but wanted to somehow fill the void missing from my life. There was an emptiness that only a good friend could fill – a real friend, someone who cares about me but also gives me pause to think about who I am. Someone who cherishes You and challenges me and keeps me on my toes. Someone . . . who I look forward to being with. Thank you, God, for giving me that friend."

CHAPTER SIX

The next day the three of us ate breakfast together. At first we were each quiet, but then a seamless transition occurred that led us to start behaving like, well, a family.

I discussed how we had tried to set a schedule for the choir director to change the music set four times a year, once each season. It just seemed like we had been singing the same hymns for years. Too boring. And there are so many great songs that we could use. I explained how, when I realized I was micromanaging, I stopped, and it made the director's job and mine so much easier.

Then Carl told me how he met with his music minister for an hour in his office every week asking what songs he should use. In a manner similar to mine, Carl realized he needed to give him his full confidence and trust and allow him to make the decision himself. Carl said it not only freed up a lot of time, it also increased the level of trust between the two of them.

Mom sat quietly eating her toast and listening to us going back and forth. I could tell she was thrilled about the progress we had made in our relationship. She knew enough not to ruin it by saying anything about it.

The next few days came and went. I said my weekend Masses and Carl presided over services at his church. I had the usual meetings with parishioners to discuss their spiritual needs. I am sure Carl did the same at his church.

After one particularly busy day I was resting in my easy chair while mom prepared supper. It was nice to have a few minutes to reflect on the day's activities. Carl returned home and after briefly exchanging pleasantries with mom came in to the living room and sat down on the couch.

"Busy day?" Carl wondered aloud.

“Oh, about the usual. Too many people with so many problems. Such is the world we live in. How are things on your side of the river?”

“About the same. Sometimes I wonder if I do any good at all. I sure cannot keep up with all the needs of my flock.”

Mom walked into the room. “I hope I am not disturbing your conversation.”

“It is okay,” I explained, “we were just arguing over who was the best baseball player of all time. I know it was Ted Williams.”

“Babe Ruth hit for power and average. And he could pitch.”

“One of us does not know what he is talking about,” I corrected.

“So glad to hear you admit it. That is the first step.”

"Well, *boys,"* – the emphasis was stinging – "enjoy beating each other's brains out. I have to finish cooking your dinner. I plan to poison at least one of your meals tonight." With that she turned and left the room.

"Why is it so hard for us to show Evie we are getting along?" Carl asked.

"I don't know, but it is a lot more fun this way."

"That, it is, John. That, it is."

We spent the next few minutes in silent reflection. Our peaceful existence was short-lived as mom came back into the room with something important to tell us.

"There's a man at the back door. He's looking for money."

I turned to Carl and let him know this was not an unusual occurrence. People from the community had a lot of pride but in these tough times they would give in and show up asking for money.

“Is it one of our parishioners?” I asked.

“No one I have ever seen. He looks like a homeless man. Or . . . what we used to call a bum.”

“Please show him in,” I said.

“Do you want to see him your office? Alone?” It was nice of her to offer that, but no longer necessary.

“It doesn’t sound like this is a Catholic issue. Carl, if you are willing, let’s both of us talk with him here.” If he was not a member of the parish there was no need to squirrel him away in my office. For all I knew, he was a Lutheran and could better interact with Carl.

"Of course. I am always happy to assist."

Mom left and returned with a young man in tow. It was immediately clear why she referred to him as a bum. He appeared to be about twenty-five years old but was so disheveled it was hard to be sure. His clothes were wrinkled and dirty. Long, greasy hair hung down to his ragged beard. Being a priest as long as I had, it was easy to size someone up quickly as to what the real issue was. The fragrance of alcohol confirmed for me what his appearance indicated.

The man was average in size and height. His manner of standing made me think he was a little off base mentally – possibly from substance abuse.

"Please pull up that chair and sit down with us. My name is Father John. This is the Reverend Carl. How may we help you?"

"I need money." He was quick and to the point. I had to give him that.

"Please, what is your name?"

"I'm not looking for conversion here, man, just some money. Are you going to give me some or not?" The man had some disordered thinking, but when it came down to it he could be very straightforward.

"We're just wondering what your name is," Carl gently stated.

"You're not going to do some 'counseling' and make me into one of your Sunday sermons. I am not interested in church or God or anything but a few bucks. Don't make me jump through any hoops by having to listen to your lectures. Do I get some or not?"

“What will you do with the money?” Whether he liked it or not, I was not going to give any of the hard-earned money our parishioners had donated to him without getting some answers.

The man rolled his eyes and looked down at his dirty, torn sneakers. Then he stared at me with no small amount of anger on his face. “Oh what the hell, man. My grandmother needs an operation. I’m going to donate it to the orphanage. I am going to buy food for kittens and puppies. Why do you make me lie to you? What do you think I’m going to do with it?”

“I appreciate the honesty.” I really did and I wanted him to know it.

“Booze or drugs?” Carl was, like me, quick to the point.

“Depends on how much you give me. Booze is cheaper, but I prefer drugs.”

I folded my hands, as much to give me a minute to think as to present a certain image. "Are you hungry?"

The man thought he had found a way to get what he wanted. "Hungry? Yeah, give me twenty bucks and I'll go buy a sandwich." He put his hand out, palm up.

"I'll ask our housekeeper to make you a sandwich. We have some leftover roast beef from last night."

More anger appeared on the man's face. "That's it? A frickin' sandwich?"

"That's the best we can do."

"Don't give me that crap, man. You church guys are loaded, super-rich, and you won't give me a nickel." His voice was rising. I began to get concerned.

We sat silently, exchanging glances. It seemed to me the man was all bluff. I calmed myself. There would be no problems here. I remained confident in spite of what he said next.

"I should kick both your asses, then take what I want. You priests are pacifists, aren't you? I could give you both such a beating." He clenched his fists.

"This day is bringing one disappointment after another to you," Carl began to educate the young man.

"What do you mean?" Carl had his attention.

"I'm not a priest. And I'm not a pacifist. And the best part is I taught boxing to kids at the community center for twenty years. I am a fast and hard puncher. Better yet, years of playing chess has taught me how to strategize. I can overwhelm an opponent in moments."

"He isn't just whistling 'Dixie' with that statement." I had tasted that of which Carl spoke.

"So you're a tough guy, eh? Well, I don't care. I am young and you are old. I can hammer you."

"Not so tough, really. But I'm pretty sure I can lay a beating on you. The best part is when I'm done I can confess my sin of violence to Father John here."

"I thought you didn't believe in confession, Carl." This conversation was turning into a rollicking good time.

Carl shrugged. "After I bounce him around this room like a rubber ball I better do something."

The man turned towards me. Now he was upset, but not at the fact that we weren't giving him money. "Are you going to let him talk like that to me? People like him are supposed to be nice."

"Oh, I'm enjoying this too much. Are you sure you couldn't take him? I am willing to put odds, very favorable odds on a match-up."

"Five to one?" Carl asked. "I am still pretty good."

"Well, Carl, given the age factor I was thinking three to one."

"Fair enough." Carl seemed satisfied.

"That's it. I'm out of here." The man got up and started walking towards the door.

"I thought you needed money," I said.

The man stopped, turned around, and glared at us.

"You're supposed to just give me some cash, and here you are screwing with me."

"Oh, I'm not offering to give you money. But you know something . . . we have a lot of yard work to do. It might be worth something.

"What kind of money?" The man was interested.

"Fifty dollars."

"I'll take it." He agreed. I could see him calculating how high he was going to be able to get.

"My profession requires I be clear. I'll give you a fifty dollar credit at the Family Restaurant in town. That's a lot of food. You can't convert it to cash."

"They serve booze there?"

"No, that's why they call it the "Family Restaurant." You should also know that I'm not stupid. Not that stupid, anyway. I do this from time to time for people in the parish. I will just make a phone call and that will take care of it."

"I guess that'll help me," he said as he scratched his beard. "Then the money I do get from begging I can use for booze."

"You see!" I exclaimed. "Everyone wins."

"You are the weirdest priest I have ever met."

"Yeah, I hear that a lot."

"What's the job?"

I stood up and walked to the window. The man followed me. I pointed to a pile of wood behind the garage.

“See that big pile of wood? We had it cut and delivered but it does no good to us out there by the garage. If you can haul it and stack it next to the house, we’ll be able to use it in our fireplace when winter comes. Not too big of a job. I bet you can be done in a couple hours. Go ahead and get started and I’ll bring out that sandwich.”

The man snorted. “I get it. An honest day’s work is going to change me, right? Make me see the light? Fat chance.” The man studied me and apparently realized this was going to be the best he could do. “Okay, I’ll do it.”

The man walked outside the house. I watched him walk to the wood pile. There was no need to supervise him. With a job like that either the wood was moved or it wasn’t. Carl rose out of his chair and walked over to the window. He looked at me and smiled.

"Hmmm. A few weeks ago you paid fifty dollars to someone to move that same pile of wood from the house to the garage. Now you're paying to move it back."

"That is well-traveled wood. I've lost count of how many times it's been moved back and forth over the years," I mused.

Carl stared out the window for a long time. I was beginning to get suspicious about this show of interest. I walked back to the window and saw the man working. Slowly but steadily, he was making a dent in the woodpile. I turned and glanced at Carl, giving him my best version of a stink-eye. Yes, even priests do that. Don't blame me, I inherited it from my mom.

Carl realized his intentions were becoming obvious. He shrugged and rubbed his chin.

"John, do you know what we have here? A captive audience. I feel a real need to engage in some evangelization. Well, this is your place, so you should have dibs. Or do you want to flip for him?"

"I have to finish a report for the Bishop, Carl. Besides, this one has *Lutheran* written all over him." I patted him on the back and headed for my office.

Carl ran to his chair and grabbed his Bible. He made a beeline for the door.

I mumbled to myself as I entered my office, "There is a man who loves a challenge."

Ninety minutes later I finished typing up my report on the spiritual needs of this part of the diocese. I had no doubt whatsoever the Bishop assigned me the occasional report just to make sure I knew he was keeping an eye on me. It really did not matter to me. I enjoyed the chance to consider theology and the real life needs of my parishioners. Needless to say I would never admit that fact to the Bishop. No need to encourage him.

Walking back into the living room I found Carl sprawled on the couch. He did not look happy.

"How did the evangelization go, Carl?"

"I don't think he will be stepping inside my church any time soon. He is really anti-everything. He does not want to hear about God, prayer or salvation. I finally gave up and came inside. I know a lost cause when I see one."

"Lost cause. Some would call that a challenge." I offered that for his consideration.

"There are challenges that I embrace, and then there are realities that I accept." Carl was being spectacularly eloquent. There was nothing more I could add.

The next day I had several appointments with parishioners, the usual fare for a man of the cloth. One woman whose husband was cheating on her, one man whose was having trouble grasping the reality of God in everyday life, an elderly man who wanted to pray with me, and a teenage girl who was doing a report on priests for her senior class paper.

I especially enjoyed meeting with the teenager. I don't think the teenage girl had ever met a priest before. Folks like that usually have some degree of trepidation. I find the best approach in these instances is to ask them a few questions about themselves. It loosens them up and puts them at ease. I must say I was very impressed with the young lady, and it gave me a great deal of hope for the future of our society and our church.

The negativity with which so many young people are viewed is not uncommon to this age but certainly troubling nonetheless. Every age has its challenges. This one is different, though. A hundred years ago young people did not have the burden of mass media constantly trying to influence them with mind-pounding cynicism and evil. That they should survive at all and maintain any semblance of the love of God is a tribute to the young.

In the midst of my musing, the telephone range. Mr. Jones's wife was dying. This was not a surprise. She was eighty-five years old and had been in failing health for several months. I grabbed my anointing materials and quickly headed to my car. I shouted my mission to mom as I left. There was no time for details. She had been through this many times. She would feed Carl dinner and keep some food warming for me in the oven. Such was the life of a priest. This was not a profession where one could work Monday through Friday and go home at five o'clock. As crazy as it sounded, I loved the hours. There was a great satisfaction in being needed and in helping people.

The event played out the way so many others have over my career. Concerned family members were met and talked with. I performed the last rites while anxious children and grandchildren stood by watching. Mr. Jones, of course, was devastated. After sixty years together, one could expect no less.

When the inevitable happened, everyone was as ready as they could be. I gave out what consolation I could. We made funeral plans and I said my goodbyes. I glanced at my watch as I walked out to my car. Four hours had passed so quickly it was hard to believe.

While I was driving home mom and Carl had some time to get to know each other. Not having me around gave them both more freedom to be themselves. It was important to me that mom felt comfortable with someone who a month ago had been a stranger to her. Things seemed to be going well for them but I thought this alone time would help with their comfort level.

Piecing together some things mom told me later and using my own knowledge of Carl's background, along with my vivid imagination, I came up with this scenario.

Mom and Carl sat in the living room, reading. After several minutes they were relaxed and comfortable. She probably looked over at him.

"Carl, can I ask you something? If you don't mind. It's one of those it's-none-of-my-business questions." Mom was no doubt hesitant with her question.

"Of course, Evie. What is it?"

"We have something in common, you and me." Mom gently led him in the conversation.

"Our spouses are gone?"

"How did you know that's what I was going to say?" Mom was genuinely surprised.

“Well, that’s one of the few things we have in common. That and affection for your son. Of course, I think you have edge on that one.”

“My John died five years ago. Johnny’s father, I mean. It was always a little confusing have two people with the same name in the family.”

“Five years. Yes. Same as my Betty.” Carl would have closed his eyes when he spoke of his dead wife. I knew that from blessing.

“How are you doing these days?” Mom was genuinely empathic.

“No one can understand what it is like unless they’ve lost the love of their life. You don’t really get over it. At least I never have. But I have learned how to deal with the pain. I guess you just get used to it.”

Mom would have bit her lip, wondering if she should ask the next question. She would have gone and ahead and asked, “You never wanted to remarry?”

“I will when you do.”

They both would have exchanged knowing looks and smiles.

“But don’t you get lonely?”

“At first I did. But then I realized . . . well, now I’m going to sound like a minister. I found such comfort and solace in God. I really felt like he was there with me during my low points. I never would have made it without Him.”

“That’s beautiful. I bet you give wonderful sermons at your church.”

Carl would have given a wink and said, "Show up this Sunday and hear for yourself."

"Ha, Johnny would never forgive me," she joked.

"And I would never let him forget it," Carl laughed.

"Honestly, when you first arrived here I thought you two were going to kill each other. Now, well, it's funny how things turn out."

"As far as a stranger invading his personal space – well, I can't say I blame him for being wary at first. As for us being of different faiths – we all believe the same thing. Just not the same way."

It was at that point that I pulled up to the house and saw through the window Mom standing and patting Carl's shoulder. If they were having a moment, I did not want to interrupt. I sat the front step and said a decade of the rosary. I then walked in and greeted the two of them.

"Well, she passed. They are really going to miss her," I informed them.

I couldn't help but notice they suddenly seemed uncomfortable. I couldn't contain myself.

"I hope I am not interrupting something?" I said with amusement.

Mom laughed. "Oh, you. Carl and I were just talking about our loss. It's been five years for both of us."

"Please don't let me stop you." The worst thing one can do when someone is blessing emotional release is to interrupt the process. I walked back into the kitchen.

"Evie, I wonder, what date did your husband die?"

"It was August 1st."

Carl was stunned. With an unusual display of emotion, he stammered, "August 1st? That's when Betty died."

Mom cried out, "How amazing! What a coincidence. John, don't you think that means something?"

"It probably does, Mom, I just don't know what," I said from my hiding place in the kitchen.

"There are no coincidences you know, John." Mom was drawing me into the conversation, so I had to re-enter the room.

"I tend to go along with Evie on this one, John." Carl made it two against one. I enjoyed the odds.

"Now I'll play the skeptic. Can you show me where it says that in the Bible? Or is that something Luther decided to throw into the mix one cold winter's day?" Weeks ago we would have talked with a sneer. Now we threw light-hearted jabs at one another – so light there was never a need to duck.

"I'm talking theology, John. We have to use our best judgment to interpret and understand the Bible."

"I sense a debate about the meaning of 'Kephas' coming up."

"What?" Mom wondered.

Carl explained it to her. "Kephas is what you Catholics claim gives the Pope his authority."

"But you know better." I smiled.

"Not me – Martin Luther." Carl assumed a professorial manner he must have learned in the seminary.

"Yeah, if you can't trust a disgruntled ex-priest who can you trust?" I reminded Carl of Luther's roots. Besides, when it came to being disgruntled, I was the resident expert.

Mom breathed the same loud sigh as when my sister and I used to go on and on. "We'll call this one a draw, boys."

"I was just getting warmed up," Carl claimed.

"I was getting more warmed up than you are." I was having too much fun.

"Do you both want to spend the next hour standing in the corner?"

"He started it!" Carl and I exclaimed in perfect harmony while pointing our fingers at each other.

At this mom shook her head and walked out of the room. Steeped in the satisfaction that only eight-year-olds and middle-aged men in need of growing up know, we open our books and quietly read – for about ten seconds. It was then I noticed Carl was reading a Bible. I was reading a western novel. This one-upmanship would not stand. I carefully considered my snappy comeback when something happened that caused me to lose my train of thought.

The back door opened and someone walked into the kitchen. I knew I had seen Mom walk down the hallway to her room. Carl was sitting across from me. That meant someone had walked into the house. My house. That bad feeling you get when you realize you should be afraid was emanating into the room. I looked over at Carl and saw a concerned look on his face. He was thinking the same thing I was. We simultaneously set our books down. Now I wished it was a Bible I had been reading. The footsteps came closer. A man walked out of the kitchen and into the living room. It was the homeless man from yesterday. We were startled to see him.

“What are you doing here?” I demanded. “You moved all the wood we had to move yesterday.” I was suspicious of his intention.

“And don’t you knock?” Carl demanded with a much sterner manner.

“I’m doing a job for Evie today. She asked me to come back. Evie said to just come in when I got here.”

That gave us both pause. We considered our situation. The man took advantage of our silence to make things worse.

"She's in charge, right? I mean, she's the boss here?" As disordered as his thinking sometimes was he seemed to be able to figure out our hierarchy.

"Ouch," Carl said, as he looked over at me.

"An astute observation." I was forced to admit the truth. I was a fifty year old man, and my mom still ran the show. As least she was subtle about it. I was determined to get something out this situation, so I pushed forth.

"Can you at least tell me your name?" I asked.

"I only give that information to my friends," he replied matter-of-factly. There was no malice in his tone.

Then the boss came down the stairs and walked into the room. She walked over to the man and smiled.

"John Paul! Thanks for coming back today," Mom said happily.

Carl and I, with so little in common, looked at each other in amazement and mouthed the words, "John Paul."

"Evie, I have the whole day to help you out. Now, where are those cabinets you need painted?"

"John Paul?" I repeated his name out loud, not to get his attention, but in the hope it would help me with the new reality. One of the people I admired more than anyone in the world had the same name as this drug-addled bum.

"Yeah?" John Paul mumbled. How I wished he had not responded to my call.

"That's your . . . real name?" I prayed this was all a mistake. As my parishioners so often tell me is the case in their lives, my prayer was not answered. I always told them the prayers would be answered but in a different way than planned. It was time to take my own bitter medicine.

"Something wrong with my name?" John Paul seemed vaguely upset.

"No, great name. Don't you think, Carl?" I was trying to be positive with the horrendous situation in which I had found myself drowning.

"I can stand it if you can." Carl's eyes were wide. He appeared almost as upset as I was. He had muttered a classic line if ever I heard one.

John Paul walked to the kitchen door and looked into the room. He shook his head.

"Wow, those cabinets are really in bad shape."

“Can you fix them?” Mom asked. I hoped his answer would be no and then he would give up and walk out.

“I want to a good job for you – do it right. I’m going to have to take them down from the wall and then carry them outside. First thing to do next is sand them. Then, I’ll prime them and paint them. This is going to take several days to complete.” Now John Paul was sounding like a totally different person, not a druggie in search of his next fix. Mom’s magic was working where my abilities had failed.

“Yep,” John Paul reaffirmed, “I’m gonna be here a long time.”

Carl and I looked at each other. We simultaneously buried out heads in our hands. John Paul walked into the kitchen. I took advantage of my ever diminishing privacy.

“Mom, would you please come here a minute?” I summoned her as nicely as I could, given everything that had transpired. I was impressed with John Paul's attitude but knew addicts could put on a convincing façade. I did not trust him.

"Yes, dear?" she replied innocently.

"Do you think when you invite unknown men into the house you might let us know? Especially manipulative, unrepentant, non-recovering drug users who have threatened to do us violence?"

"Okay." Mom shrugged and walked away.

"John, I think your intervention failed."

"It's been fifty years of failed interventions."

Just as I was beginning to find some peace in my circumstances John Paul walked back into the living room to spread some more of his special sunshine.

"Hey, man – where do you keep your tools? I need a screwdriver and some other stuff."

"Let me try to understand this. You contract to do a job and you expect the customer to provide the tools?"

John Paul nonchalantly replied, "Well, yeah. Do you want this done or don't you?"

I sighed with resignation. "What else would anyone expect? Go out into the garage. On the back wall I keep a tool chest. You'll find what you need there."

"Thanks, man," John Paul said as he sauntered off.

I realized I had to protect what little assets my parish had. "John Paul, please don't take offense but the tools are old and not worth much."

“What, you think I’m going to steal them and buy drugs?” John Paul asked, without anger.

“You are an active drug user aren’t you?” I hoped I wouldn’t have to explain my concern.

“Yeah, so?” John Paul innocently and honestly responded.

“And you have no money to buy drugs?” This conversation was tiring me out.

“What’s your point, man?” John Paul showed some irritation. He seemed to want me to get to the point.

“Apparently there is no point in trying to make a point. Could you please at least call me “Father” instead of “man”?”

“You’re not my father. How about if I call you John?”

"That's what I call him." Carl interjected. I glared at him and he smiled back. It was hard to be angry at him. John Paul, on the other hand, made it easy.

"I really would prefer you call me 'Father.' It is a title."

John Paul seemed to consider it. He put his hand to his chin. He shook his head.

"I'll be honest, I don't see it happening." John Paul turned and left the house.

"Intervention-wise, you're 0 for 2 today, John."

"And it is still the morning. Who knows how many times I can strike out by supper time?"

Mom came back in the room. It was obvious she wanted to talk to me.

"I think that deep down John Paul is really a nice young man," Mom told me.

"My view of deep down must be blocked by that scruffy beard," I explained.

"I brought him some lemonade while he was stacking wood. We got to talking for quite a while. The poor boy has had a difficult life. He said his father never seemed to care much for him."

"Imagine that," I offered.

Mom was unhappy with my response. Now came the crossed arms and a dirty look.

"I asked him back today because I thought being around two holy, mature men would be a good influence."

"How is it working out so far?" Carl impishly inquired.

"I just need to find two holy, mature men." Neither of us dared respond so she again left us alone.

"You know, Evie has such a pleasant way of insulting us that I don't half mind."

I nodded my agreement.

"With mom it's a mixed bag. Half the time I don't know how to take what she says. One of the first sermons I ever gave, I lost my place halfway through it. It was embarrassing. Mom came up to me after Mass and said, 'Don't worry, John. Nobody noticed. Most of the people fell asleep after the first minute of the homily anyway.'"

"Hmmm, do you ever wonder where you got your sense of humor?" Carl pondered.

"It's good I have someone to blame, I guess."

Carl paused while considering his next statement. He had a way of being very thoughtful about things that mattered a lot to him.

"Ah, yes. I envy you your mother. Mine died right before I graduated from divinity school. It was her dream to see me become a minister. I take some solace in the fact that she knew it was going to happen."

"I find having lost my father actually helps me comfort those who have lost a loved one. Do you feel that way, too?" I enjoyed these conversations. It was good to have someone in a similar profession to share things with.

"Absolutely. Unfortunately, it's one of those things you can't understand unless you've been there."

We sat there silently mulling our commonality. Of course, it did not last long. John Paul entered the room, tools in hand.

"You guys want to give me a hand?" John Paul was serious.

"NO!" we replied, in perfect harmony.

"Aren't you dudes supposed to help your fellow man?" Now John Paul was trying to guilt us. He was an amateur dealing with professionals. I would put this to rest.

"Are you being paid for this?" I reminded him.

"You think I'd do this for free?" John Paul asked incredulously.

"That thought would never cross my mind."

"Evie made the same deal with me that you did. I'm gonna eat like a king for a long time to come."

Mom came back onto the room. It appeared she was looking for John Paul, not us.

"John Paul, did you find everything you need?"

"Yes, Evie. No problem. I found the bed frame too."

"Bed frame?" I did not know what this meant, but I was sure I wouldn't like it.

"John Paul is homeless," Mom explained. "He doesn't have anywhere to sleep. I told him we had a spare bedroom but he said he would be more comfortable sleeping in the garage. I told him he can carry out the mattress in the last remaining bedroom."

"You told him he could live here, on this property?"

"I'm just following my Lord's example. Maybe you should try it."

John Paul decided to make an unpleasant confrontation worse. "Don't have a spaz, man. It's not like I'm going to do any drugs while I'm here."

Carl jumped in feet first. "Why live in the garage? Why not the house?"

"No offense, man. But those collars you wear really freak me out."

Carl and I examined each other. Our collars were who we were and told the world what we did. It had never occurred to us that our collars could signify anything bad. I responded with sarcasm.

"Sorry our appearance is so offensive to you," I gently mocked.

"It's getting easier. I figure after a few days living here, hanging out, and eating meals with you, I'll be cool."

"Hanging out?" Carl said, mouth agape.

"Eating meals with us?" I was about to go on a rant. Mom came to the rescue. I should say she stopped me from saying something inappropriate. Sometimes my mouth said things before my mind had filtered my words through the Ten Commandments.

"You don't expect John Paul to walk all the way to the restaurant for all his meals, do you?"

"The exercise might do him good," Carl offered. I was glad he was at least trying to be helpful.

John Paul tired of the conversation and walked into the kitchen.

Mom spoke quietly. “After all, he might run into the wrong element if he goes into downtown to eat.”

“You’re right, of course.” I hated it when mom instructed me. I especially hated it when she was right.

“Well . . . ” I gave in. “Jesus ate with sinners.”

“And John Paul will eat with you two.”

“Wait,” Carl asked, “are you equating us with Jesus or the sinners?”

“Think what you want to, dears.”

Mom sat down on the couch and started reading. I decided to leave for my office and work on my sermon.

Carl thought I was going to work on something else. “Are you going to take a turn with John Paul?”

“What do you mean?”

“I have tried to evangelize the faith to our new friend. No progress at all. I thought maybe you were going to take stab at it. Make lemonade out of lemons, so to speak.”

“What has he told you?”

“He doesn’t want anything to do with religion.”

“He doesn’t mind taking our money, though. Or eating our food.”

“There is some inconsistency there, yes.” Carl smiled.

“Let’s think about this a little bit. Someone once told me that many mental health problems could be cured or at least made better if one would accept God into their lives. The same is probably true for chemical health issues. John Paul has both mental health and chemical abuse issues. His thinking is disordered which is probably due to his addictions. I think the only way to get him off of drugs is to substitute God.

John Paul walked through the room, a tool in one hand and a sandwich in another. He munched on the food on his way to the bathroom.

"Hmm," I observed. "It appears food might be something of a substitute, too."

"I hope he leaves some roast beef for a snack. We Lutherans aren't into fasting like you Catholics are."

"If John Paul stays here very long, we'll be past fasting and well into famine."

A few days came and went. Somehow, I guess through the grace of God, I was able to get used to John Paul and his constant wandering through the house. There was never a need to tell him to make himself at home in the kitchen or bathroom. I guess you can get used to anybody if you pray hard enough.

CHAPTER SEVEN

A particularly tough schedule faced me this week. Parishioners had the usual assortment of issues, but a few were extraordinary. I will try my best to accurately reflect what went on without, of course, using names or comments that could identify who the people are.

My ten o'clock appointment (we have a standing weekly meeting) with Mrs. Kathy Johnson went, as best I can recall, like this:

"Father, have you given any more thought to the request I made last week?"

"You mean the one where you wanted me to give a homily accusing the mayor, governor, and anyone who disagrees with you politically of being the devil?" I just wanted to make sure I had it right.

"Yes, that's it." Mrs. Johnson brightly beamed. "Will you do it?"

"No." There was no need for more verbiage.

"So you're on their side?"

"I'm not on anyone's side. The pulpit is not for preaching politics."

"Whose ridiculous rule is that?"

"The Pope's," I matter-of-factly said, hoping that would end the conversation.

"Maybe I should contact him," she declared, excited at her idea.

"Yes, maybe you should." I felt sorry for His Eminence but with luck he would never know I foisted her on him.

We sat there and exchanged pleasantries for a few more minutes. That is when she dropped the bomb.

"Father, there's one more thing."

I silently gasped and steeled myself for what was coming.

"Do you know anything about adultery?"

"Well, not first hand." Fortunately, I was able to plead ignorance.

We stared at each other for another minute.

"Is there something you want to . . . confess to, Mrs. Johnson?"

The slow change of expression on her face could have been timed with a calendar. Finally she understood what I was saying.

“ME? ME? Are you asking if I have been cheating on my dear Bennie?”

“Well, Mrs. Johnson, I frankly do not have any idea what you are trying to tell me.” And that was the truth.

“It is not me. I think my neighbor, Janie Mahoney, is cheating on her husband.”

I sighed. “Please, Mrs. Johnson, no names.”

“But that is her name,” she protested.

“Okay, first of all, this is gossip. Which is sinful. We should not talk about what someone might or might not be doing. Second, if you must say something like that to me, do not include her name.” Apparently my years of preaching had had no effect. Another person who practiced unconsciousness when I spoke from my pulpit.

"But I am not being sinful. I am not the one committing adultery. I am only trying to help."

Now she had my interest. "Please explain how you are trying to help."

"Well, I have been logging Janie's suspicious behavior for a month now. I wanted to share it with you to see what you think."

"You lost me at logging."

"You know," Mrs. Johnson abruptly said, apparently upset that I was not following the conversation, "writing down suspicious things. She comes and goes at all hours of the day and night."

"And, being retired like you are, you spend a lot of time looking out the window? Checking on this Janie?"

"Well, not just her, of course," she corrected.

"You log other neighbors' activities as well?"

"How else will I keep track of what is going on?"

"Is it your responsibility to know what your neighbors are doing?"

"Am I not my brother's keeper?" Mrs. Johnson asked, getting all the more upset with me.

"The Bible does say you are his keeper, but not his snooper."

That comment, unfortunately, seemed to go over her head.

"Well, anyway, I see her coming and going at all hours. Her husband works long hours so he must not know anything about it. She could be up to anything while he is gone."

"Again, none of our business." I wondered how many times I would have to repeat that for it to sink in.

"So it is okay with you if my neighbor is off having illicit sex with other men?"

Her comment was too awful to respond to directly.

"Have you considered getting a hobby? Something to keep you busy during the day?"

"Oh my, no! I just don't have any time for a hobby."

"I think a hobby would be a good idea. Another good idea would be for you to quit spying on your neighbor."

"I am not spying."

"Quite seriously here, Mrs. Johnson, if you persist in nosing into other people's business, you will need to confess this to me."

"Confess? Don't you understand I have not done anything?"

"Gossiping about your neighbor. Thou shalt not lie. It is pretty plain now, isn't it?"

"Well, I think I need to go home now."

"Very well, Mrs. Johnson. Please consider what I said."

The next two appointments went better. A grieving widow wanting to talk about her feelings. Then a mother whose son refused to attend church. There was nothing special in what I said or did for them. Anyone could do what I did. It was just a matter of being there for someone.

My last appointment of the day had me feeling anxious. The parishioner was a thirty-year-old man, an auto mechanic by profession. He came in and shook my hand with a crushing grip. I was tall, just over six feet and of average build but this man made me look small by comparison. He was easily six-foot-five and a beefy two hundred and fifty pounds. His strength no doubt came in handy on his job. What intrigued me about this guy, though, was not his physical prowess. It was his intellect.

The man, I'll refer to him here as Steve, got married a year ago. His wife was a practicing Catholic but his family had never attended a church of any kind and, outside of the occasional funeral or attending a friend's wedding, he had never set foot in a church.

Catholics who intend to marry must meet with the parish priest several times before he performs the ceremony. Steve was noticeably uncomfortable at our first meeting. I tried to engage him in conversation, but since he was reluctant to participate, I spent most of the time discussing faith and wedding plans with Julie, his fiancée.

The second meeting was much like the first. I knew he felt most comfortable as an observer and respected that. Towards the end of our third meeting things appeared to be going smoothly. We planned a standard Catholic wedding, Mass and all. We agreed any children would be raised as Catholics. I again did the requisite bringing up of whether Steve wanted anyone representing a non-Catholic clergy in attendance. Of course, he did not, so there were no issues there. But what happened then changed things.

"Well, Steve and Julie," I began, "since things are going so well, I am not sure we need to meet again. We are all in agreement about the wedding and the usual agreements. We will meet again of course the week of the wedding for rehearsal. Please have the florist contact me with any questions. Also, since you plan on having a musician from out of town come in, I need to talk with her briefly. So that is that."

I looked at Julie and she appeared pleased. One less meeting to go is always welcome. Brides are plenty busy and I was happy to give her a break. I glanced over at Steve and was surprised to see him shaking his head.

"That's it?" Steve asked. He appeared to be taken aback. I thought he would be pleased.

"Well," I stated, "we have agreed on everything, so we are done." Then sense kicked into me as I realized there must be an issue I did not know about. "Perhaps I have left something undone?"

"I thought you were, you know, going to try to convert me." Steve seemed embarrassed to be saying this. "I have been waiting for the hard sell or the subtle approach or whatever method you use. I am sorry to say I guess I thought you were going to do something. The fact is I am very happy you did not."

“Well, we discussed religion at our first meeting. You said, I think, that you grew up without religion and had no desire to adopt one now. I did say if you ever had any questions about Catholicism you were welcome to ask.” As I said this, I realized something was going on in his head.

“Is it too late to ask now?” This was another question I did not anticipate.

“No, not too late at all.” I looked at Julie as I said this and saw that she seemed as puzzled as me.

“Steve, now is a good time to ask,” I prompted him.

“What about being Catholic is different than other religions? And why do you believe in Jesus? And what is it with bread being Jesus? That does not make any sense to me at all. And – ”

I motioned for him that I needed to interrupt.

"Steve, one question at a time, please. Those are all good questions. And I suspect you have dozens more. Each of those questions is going to take a while to answer. Could we please schedule some more meetings to discuss them?"

"Look, Father. I will be clear. I am not converting. I have zero interest in being a Catholic. Since Julie is a Catholic and she believes all these things, I just want to know what your faith is all about. After all, she is going to be my wife, and I want to know as much about her as I can. Since religion is a big part of her life, I think I should understand it. Does that make sense to you?"

"Yes, Steve. Knowing as much about one's spouse as you can is smart and shows you really want to have a solid marriage. This sacrament is about being a partner and as close spiritually as you will be emotionally and physically."

"There's that word again. Sacrament. Maybe we should start there," Steve suggested.

"Yes, that would be a good place to start. I have my calendar here. Let's see what time and days work for you."

All those thoughts of a year ago flashed by in the time it took Steve to sit in his chair and look at me. He seemed to be suppressing a smile.

"You know why I am here, Father?" he asked.

"We have a standing meeting the first Wednesday of each month." I was eager to know where this was going but did not want to appear overly anxious.

"I remember," Steve began what was to be a lengthy statement, "when we first met. I did not trust you. I thought you were going to try to talk me into converting. I have a couple friends who converted to their wife's religion when they married. They knew nothing about the faith, they just did it to keep their wives happy. I can't tell you how stupid I think that is."

I nodded. Steve was perceptive. These kinds of conversions frequently don't work well. The spouse who converts only to please their betrothed seldom becomes a regular church goer. The conversion is more of a burden to be carried and sometimes leads to marital discord as the person's obvious disinterest in their new religion can be a point of contention.

Steve continued, "I tried to learn everything about Julie I could. I think that is important if you want a marriage to work. She loves golf. I went golfing with her quite a few times. It is not my sport, but from going around the course with her, I understand now why she enjoys it so much. That great drive you make, that long putt you sink. It can be very satisfying. Plus she is in a league and gets to socialize with her friends. It is a lot of fun for her and now I get it."

I nodded. Sometimes the best thing a priest can do is keep his mouth tightly shut.

"So I did what you told me to when we first met. I always thought Jesus was probably a fictional character but I did my own research like you said. There is a lot of historical evidence showing Jesus existed."

Nodding was working for me, so I did not change doing so.

"And then once that was resolved I took on the big question – was Jesus who He said He was? I tried to prove He wasn't. I couldn't do so. Didn't that bother you that I tried so hard to prove Jesus was a fraud?"

It was time for me to interject a little shock to his system. "I did the same thing."

Steve's eyes got as wide as a kid's opening an unexpected Christmas present. "YOU?"

I nodded once more. "As a teenager I was rebellious. Those who know me would not be surprised by that. I was determined to find out for myself and make my own decision. My conclusion, after a lot of research and thought, was the same as yours. Which is good, considering my profession." I winked at him.

Steve laughed. "Yes, it would be tough for a priest to be an atheist."

We had a moment of quiet. Steve was just catching his breath.

"But then it all snowballed. If you accept one part, you have to accept another. And then another. If you accept Jesus existed and that He is God, you have to accept that everything He said is true. So when Jesus said the bread and wine became His body and blood – it must be so. When Jesus told His priests – the apostles - that they should recreate the Last Supper, and had the power to forgive sins – it must be so."

"Your logic is right on, Steve."

"I could go all night but you know how it works better than I do, Father."

Again, we had a few seconds of silence. Steve was bursting to say something. The fuse was lit, I was not going to say anything to snuff it out.

"So, when can we make it right?" Steve asked.

"Make it right?" Steve had a habit of saying phrases I did not understand.

"I want to join the church. I want, no, I *need* to be a Catholic."

A giant smile came across my face. I reached across the desk and shook his hand.

"I will sign you up for RCIA. It's a series of classes for adults who want to be Catholics. We'll bring you into the church at the Easter Vigil Mass."

"I can't wait," Steve said excitedly.

We walked merrily to the front door and Steve reached out to shake my hand again. It was so rewarding to see someone ecstatic about joining the faith. I said goodbye and turned to see Mom walking out of the kitchen.

"Mom, you will never guess what just happened with Steve!" I wanted to share my good news.

"He told you he was converting to Catholicism." She responded matter-of-factly.

"How did you know that?"

"How could you not know that? Have you not seen the change in him? Whenever I bump into him at the store he seems much more content. And he has been attending Mass with Julie. You can see the Holy Spirit shining in him."

A long moment passed. Mom looked at me with that special "Mom" look.

"You *can* see, can't you?"

A true damned if you do, damned if you don't situation. If I admitted I could not, I was admitting to being a substandard priest. If I claimed I could, her Mom radar would pinpoint me as a liar, and then there would be "the lecture." The coward's way had much appeal and I chose it. Silently, I sat in my chair and grabbed the remote control and turned on the television.

CHAPTER EIGHT

Finally we had a little peace and quiet. A nice, quiet day of paying bills and catching up on paperwork was followed by a chance to watch a little baseball. Carl, who was bearable to sit with when his beloved team was not playing, and Mom, and I spent the latter part of the afternoon watching our Minnesota ballplayers knock the ball out of the stadium. We heard the back door open, and I recognized the footsteps of John Paul. He sauntered into the living room and sat on the couch next to Mom. Carl and I turned our attention from the game to study John Paul. He seemed engrossed in the game, as was Mom. There is nothing like inviting oneself into a family. Being a Catholic, and especially being a priest, I had to welcome everyone. Still, I felt a need for a process.

"Are you done with the cabinets, John Paul?" I began with a simple question.

“Yeah, man,” replied John Paul without taking his gaze from the television. “I finished those yesterday.”

Carl joined the intervention. “Is there something else you are going to be working on here?”

John Paul did not respond until the pitcher had struck out the side. Then he simply stated, “Nope, all done, man.”

Mom, always reluctant to say anything about a delicate matter, looked over at Carl and myself and shook her head. It was obvious she wanted us to be quiet. After fifty years I trust it was no surprise to her that I was not going to shut my mouth until I wanted. John Paul continued doing what he did best, being oblivious to the ongoing world, and stared at the television.

“I told John Paul he could keep living here,” Mom said gently, but with great assertion.

"I've been a priest for twenty years and I have never excommunicated anyone. Until now." My assertion was also great, though nowhere near as gentle.

"What is your problem?" Mom demanded. "His family won't have anything to do with him. We are all he has."

If anyone was living in my reality, I would not discuss this type of matter in front of him, but John Paul was off in his own universe. "Family? He is a member of our family?"

"I'm glad you understand. As Catholics we celebrate the fact that everyone is family. But I don't have to tell you that, do I, Father John?"

Ouch. Whenever mom pulled out the "Father John" routine she was serious. But so was I.

"All I understand is a few months ago I had a content, happy life. Now it seems like we're running an adult orphanage for malcontents."

"Takes one to know one, dear." With that she smiled. I don't know how she could talk so strictly and look so beautiful with her loving smile.

I turned to look at Carl. His face earnestly expressed an interest in the matter. He respectfully remained silent, recognizing this was something Mom and I had to work out between ourselves. I then turned and watched John Paul. He sat relaxed, watching a commercial on the television. His innocent, unassuming manner was childlike. I recalled clearly what Jesus told us about loving children. I could feel my brow unfurrow and my face soften.

"Well, Johnny, what do you want to do? It is your decision." Mom's submission made my way all the more obvious. I walked behind John Paul and put my hand on the back of his chair. He turned his head to look at me.

"I think we should thank God for the blessings he has bestowed on us." A strong sense of peace fell over me and, I suspect, the entire family. I sat down and we all enjoyed the game. I could not help but notice a loving smile on Mom's face.

CHAPTER NINE

Another week went by. John Paul kept busy. When we ran out of projects, he spent his time fixing up his place in the garage. I ordered some insulation and dry wall so he would actually have a room as opposed to just having a cot next to my car. He easily made the transition to eating his meals with us in the kitchen. The remaining problem was getting him to use the shower every day. He made use of the bathroom, although I suspect sometimes he just went outside behind our lilac bushes. Regardless, ever since I learned to treat the uncontrollable events in my life as an adventure, it was all working out.

At the end of the day I was putting the finishing touches on Mom's casserole because she had to run out and pick up a few items at store. Carl came home from work and appeared to be especially worn out. It seemed best to lay off the Lutheran jokes for the time.

“Everything okay, Carl?” I queried, though I knew the answer would be no. “Fix you a gin and tonic?”

“Tough day saving souls,” Carl shared. “I don’t want to drink alone. Care to pour yourself some of that healthy white wine you like and sit down?”

Mom and I enjoyed the same type of wine. That was convenient. Carl enjoyed a glass of gin every so often, so we started keeping a bottle in the cupboard. I poured us each our preferred libation and sat down.

Using my most empathic look I tried to silently encourage him to give forth. We shared a unique bond. Day after day we listened to our flock pour out their hearts. By listening to these tragic stories we unburdened our parishioners but burdened ourselves. The psychological stress a priest or minister endures is real and sometimes puts “Men of God” in a sea of stress. We had no one to share these events with as we were forbidden to repeat what we heard to any non-clergy. My mom was closer to me than anyone but I could never share the personal difficulties my parishioners would unload on me. We were permitted to consult and collaborate with a fellow clergyman, but until now neither Carl nor I had had that option. We were both reluctant to broach the subject, but today I knew I had to take the lead in making myself available to this good man.

I tried to make eye contact with Carl, but he kept staring at his glass of gin. Thousands of times I had started conversations with parishioners when I saw they did not know how to begin. This time was different. This time it was more than a parishioner, it was my friend.

"Carl, sometimes I have had have a good day, and then it would change because of one person who turned the day on its head."

Carl smiled and nodded. Now he looked me in the eye.

"I guess you know how it is, John. That is exactly what happened. It is okay to discuss this with you, isn't it?"

"We are not gossiping, Carl. It is one professional discussing a matter with another professional."

"Well, I'm afraid it is going to be a bit more complicated than that, my friend."

Now he had me curious. "Please, tell me about it."

Carl took a sip of his drink. My drink was still untouched. I had the notion that I needed to be one hundred percent clear-headed for what was to come.

"You have a parishioner named Mrs. Satane?"

"Oh no." A sinking feeling took hold and began dragging me down through the floor to the center of the earth. "Yes, she is a parishioner."

"Well, she came to see me. She is thinking of joining my church. To make it clear, she would convert from Catholicism to being a Lutheran."

If anyone else had told me that, my first reaction would have been one of ecstasy. But seldom did life work out so well. I braced myself for what was to come.

"It seems, John, she thinks you are the devil. She had a list of complaints about you as long as my arm. Now you know as well as me that no one in our business can ever please everyone. Every Sunday when we preach from the pulpit there are those who are pleased and those who are angry. Either we offended someone because we didn't talk enough about sin or we talked too much about it."

Carl took a deep breath. He seemed to be about to take a drink but thought differently and pushed his glass away.

"Well of course I welcomed Mrs. Satane but when she explained to me that she wanted to join my church not because of the basic tenants of our faith but because of her anger towards you I became reluctant. It seemed like she was doing this to get back at you somehow. As if her leaving your church would hurt you."

I tried hard not to laugh at the idea of good news hurting me.

"Then what happened?"

"After I informed her that while she was welcome she should first consider the faith, not the man standing on the pulpit, her attitude changed. She came in smiling and excited, but then she started making snide remarks. Things like 'I thought you were going to be a holy man' and 'I guess this is why no one in town ever says a good thing about you.' It seemed she was not interested in discussion but in wounding me."

"I understand." And I did. More than he knew.

"Well, I am not a psychologist but my training is that when counseling is not effective it is best to suggest the person contact a mental health professional.

"Oh no!" I knew Carl had done the right thing and paid the price for it.

"So I told her that we should end our appointment because she did not really appear to want to convert to the Lutheran Church. With that she unleashed some foul, very inappropriate language. She accused me of conspiring with you to gain revenge on her. I told her you had never discussed her with me and she screamed at me that I was a liar. She shouted, 'Liar,' at me several times. Anyone who would lose control like that isn't right in the head.

So, as I said, I told her I was not going to able to assist her but maybe someone at the Nicollet County Mental Health Clinic could help her deal with her anger."

I shook my head in sympathy.

"Then she stood up and continued to scream at me. She shouted that I was victimizing her and in on a plot against her. She was so out of control I left my seat and walked around her and opened my office door. I am very lucky that my part-time office assistant was working today. My assistant was already on her way to my office because she could hear all the shouting. When I opened the door Mrs. Satane walked up behind me and slapped the back of my head. My assistant told her not to hit me anymore, and Mrs. Satane stated that she had not done so. When my assistant said she saw her do it, Mrs. Satane stated that I had forced her to do so."

"A very good thing she was working today," I agreed.

"I know. It is hard to say what Mrs. Satane would have accused me of if we had been alone. I do not need a career-ending baseless accusation. This way I have a witness that I was assaulted. Do you think I will be all right?"

"I have known Mrs. Satane for a long time. She has no guts to publicly say anything that she knows is a lie."

Carl seemed relieved with that statement, but then I had to finish the thought.

"That is not to say that she won't do something quietly to discredit you."

"My concerns, exactly. All these years ministering to my flock, I have had many disagree with me, but never has my reputation been defamed."

“She may contact the elders in your church. She has contacted my Bishop about me.”

“He stood up for you I am sure.” A valid assumption, though I had reservations.

“More or less.” I smiled. No need to go into my past struggles. This was about Carl.

“What do you think I should do?” Carl wondered.

“Document everything in writing. And your office assistant should do it too. As soon as possible. Then you should have it dated and notarized.”

“So if she brings this up in a month or a year, I have this.” Carl shook his head. “Never thought I would have to do something like that.”

“Again,” I cautioned, “she is not likely to do anything publicly. It is possible she will make accusations about you behind your back. Most people will not believe a word of it – thanks to your reputation. Gossip about priests and ministers is not uncommon. Who knows what crazy stories circulate about me in this parish? All I do is keep doing my job. It is easy to tell you not to worry but difficult in practice.”

“I’m going to take your advice. It is good advice. I always tell my folks worry is a waste of time. Now I have to take some of my own advice.”

We sat quietly for moment. At first I thought everything was fine. Then I noticed something was still bothering Carl. He seemed uneasy, as if he wanted to say something but could not. I knew him well enough to push him a little.

“What else, Carl? What else?”

"Would you pray with me about this?"

I was caught completely off guard. My face probably showed it.

"Pray not just for my reputation. Pray that I can continue ministering God's will to my flock. And most of all, pray for Mrs. Satane."

With his last statement, it would have been impossible for me to remain a priest had I refused.

"Of course," I said, as I sheepishly realized I should have been praying for Mrs. Satane myself.

Carl surprised me once again by falling from his chair to his knees. I joined him. The hard linoleum floor of the kitchen felt oddly inviting. The realization that for the first time in my life I was going to be led in prayer by a Lutheran minister forced a humbleness on me that I desperately needed.

Carl was eloquent as he voiced his intimate plea to God. He obviously had a deep, abiding faith. We spent several minutes in prayer and finished with a moment of silence. As we got up I looked with admiration on Carl. I resolved to give extra thanks to God that night in my prayers.

CHAPTER TEN

It was another Wednesday evening and that meant Catechism class. Normally, I let the teachers run the classes without any interference from me. We had a very competent Religious Education Coordinator. She took good care of the teachers, and students always seemed to learn a lot about their faith. A couple times a year I did stop by the classes to say hi to the kids. One never knew what one would hear from the kids. It was always fun for me. I hoped they got something out of my appearance.

Tonight I decided to put the first-graders at the top of my list. Due to declining enrollments from the decrease in the number of young adults in the area, we had need of only one classroom for these little ones.

Shirley Glass was the teacher for the first-graders. She greeted me with a warm smile when I entered the room.

"Children," Shirley exclaimed, "say hello to Fr. Krentz!"

"Hello, Father!" twenty first-graders shouted. I loved their excitement and enthusiasm. Well-mannered little kids can still be loud little kids.

"Hello, class," I replied, much more quietly but still with great enthusiasm.

I started by leading the class in prayer. We did the "Our Father" and finished with a "Hail Mary." The kids knew the prayers very well, an indication of good kids and a great teacher.

"Your class knows their prayers quite well, Mrs. Glass," I complimented her.

"Thank you, Father," she replied.

“I have many other classes to visit tonight, kids. But before I go, I want to know if you have any questions for me.” I wanted the kids to feel comfortable talking with me. They seldom had contact with me, and this would be a great way for them to develop a healthy relationship with a priest.

Several hands went up. This is why I loved little kids. They had no qualms about anything. They had not yet aged to the point where they worried about what their classmates thought.

An eager little girl shot her hand up so fast I had to call on her first. I was dying to know what she was going to ask.

“Father,” she began, “how old are you?” She caught me off guard with this, but little kids always surprised when they shared what was on their minds.

“I am fifty years old,” I admitted. “I have been a priest exactly half my life – twenty-five years.”

She was not done. Her hand stayed up.

"Are you worried about dying soon?" She clarified when she saw my puzzled expression, "Because you are so old."

I heard Mrs. Glass muffling a laugh. It was important not to appear upset to this little darling.

"Well, dear, I don't think too much about death. I try to think about life instead. Every day of our life we should try to behave in a manner that pleases God. He is the one who gave us life, and the right thing to do is thank Him by doing what we should. None of us knows how long we will live, so we should appreciate every moment." I finished with a smile. These kids were experts at reading faces and expressions. I wanted to make sure everything I did with these students was positive.

Another hand rocketed skyward. I called on a little boy.

“Have you ever seen God?” he asked, with all innocence.

“No, I have not,” was the only honest possible answer. He raised his hand again.

“Then how do you know He exists? My mom says to pray to Him but I have trouble doing it because I can’t see Him.”

This little boy was saying something that people of all ages thought. This is why little children are such blessings. It was easy to see why Jesus so enjoyed sitting with children. He knew how wonderful they were.

“You are right that we cannot see God. No one can. We will see him someday, though, when we meet Him in heaven. We know we will see Him and be with Him.” My answer did not seem as good as his question deserved. “You know, too, son, there are many things that are very real that we cannot see.”

"Like what?" He was holding my feet to the fire.

"Does your mother love you?" I didn't want him to feel alone so put the question to the entire class. "Does your mother love you?"

"YES!" the kids exclaimed.

"And you love your mothers?"

"Yes!" again they answered.

"Can you see love?" I wondered.

This quieted them down. You could see the wheels working in their minds. I would add to their thoughts.

"How about air? Can you see air?"

The kids shook their heads no. Their minds were at work. This felt like a good evening's work. After this, they asked a variety of questions. I saw that fifteen minutes had gone by, and it was time to move on.

My next scheduled class was the confirmation class. I never knew what to expect with this group. Some years the kids were eager to talk with me and voice their questions. Sometimes we had great discussions about any number of things. And then there were those years when the kids sat quietly and never said a word. It seemed a matter of chance as to what would happen. It was not unusual for one or two of the kids to think it was not cool to embrace religion. They would try what they thought was shocking to the class by saying they did not believe in God or some equally unimaginative statement. I took solace in the fact that kids did things like this and most of them grew out of it in a short time. It was those few who could not admit that they were wrong and carried these hateful ideas into adulthood that concerned me. Because of their youth, they did not realize that adults have heard all the nonsense before and nothing they could exclaim about the follies of religion or the appeal of atheism was new.

I opened the door to the confirmation class; Mr. Bois was the teacher. Inside I found eighteen students evenly split in gender. The girls, as one would expect, were usually more subdued and polite. But things change, as I was soon to discover.

I greeted Mr. Bois, and he kindly introduced me to the class. Most of them looked me over carefully. In the back row a young girl turned to a gum smacking boy and chuckled. Ten seconds had passed and I felt I had sized up the problem kids already.

Two minutes later I had given a brief talk about how important they were to the future of the church and how it was my job to be available for them on their faith journey. I then asked if there were any questions. The two kids in the back row looked at each other and snickered. There were no takers to my solicitation for questions so I started with the first student and asked him a question.

"What do you think about the need to go to Mass every week?"

"It is hard to do," the student honestly answered.

"Really? Tell me why?" I really wanted to know.

"I don't know, Father. It is hard to do with all my activities."

"Oh, what kind of things are you involved in?" This kind of response is how one gets the ball rolling.

"Hockey, mostly. We have games Saturday night and it is hard to get up early to go to Mass. My mom insists we do."

"What is your name?"

"Pete."

"Pete, where did you get your athletic ability?"

Pete thought for a minute. "My dad, I guess. He never played hockey but was an athlete."

"Well, let us look at the bigger picture," I said, while trying to think how best to get my point across. "I think that your ability is a gift from God. As your dad's ability was a gift from God. All our abilities and talents are gifts from God. Going to Mass is a wonderful way to say thank you to God for everything He has given you."

"Ah, yeah, I guess." Pete gave a half-hearted agreement like kids tend to do.

“Everything good is a gift from God. Once we realize that, our lives make more sense.”

Now I was preaching, and that usually ended all discussion. I zipped my lips. A girl raised her hand.

“Yes, please tell me your name and your question.”

“My name is Catherine. Father, is there a guy living with you who is not a Catholic?”

The best conversations usually started off topic and this was no exception.

“Yes, his name is Carl and he is a Lutheran minister.”

“My mom says he should not be there.”

“Why does she say that?” I wondered to her.

"Because he's a prophet of a false religion." She was obviously parroting what her mom told her.

"Well, I think the Reverend Carl is a fine man and will probably get to heaven before I do," I countered.

"Then why be a Catholic?" She asked a valid question given my statement.

"Jesus started our religion. It is the only religion he started. It fully conveys His truth, and we get the entire benefit of all the sacraments. On the other hand, it is the individual's embrace of the faith that makes the difference."

She shook her head while she tried to sort out what I said. "That means that, even though you have the benefit of being a Catholic, the Lutheran guy could make better use of what he knows about Jesus than you do?"

“Your insight is excellent.” I praised her.

“So you are admitting you are not a good person?” She was astonished.

“I am not as good a person as I could be,” I stated frankly. “With the graces Jesus has bestowed on me through Catholicism, I could be much better than I am.”

This seemed to instill some thought into the kids. Most of the kids. While the majority of the kids were deep in thought about what I said the two in the back were getting louder and more disruptive. Mr. Bois hushed them.

The boy nodded to the girl and she smiled at him, then turned towards me and raised her hand.

“Yes,” I said, what is your question?”

“Father, why does the church hate gays and women?” she said, while failing to hide a smirk.

“What makes you think such a silly thing is true?” I found that asking for examples was helpful, at least to the innocent bystanders who sat uncomfortably. The other kids seemed to dread this girl speaking up.

“Well, everyone knows the church hates gays,” she exclaimed.

“Everyone? I don’t know it. Most people I know do not feel that way. Be careful with speaking sweeping generalities.” I was setting her up. Again, I felt there was little I could do to change her immature thought process, but I believed I could comfort the rest of the class with some truth.

“Why then,” she continued, “won’t you let gays in your church?”

"Well, first of all, it is not my church. The church belongs to everyone. The definition of the word Catholic means universal and that means everyone is welcome in it. So there is your 'everyone.' Second, since some of our parishioners are gay, some openly so, and they attend Mass every Sunday, I wonder why you say I will not let them in. I also wonder if you realize you are being manipulated to say things that are not true."

She was puzzled by this and did what kids like her do – she looked to the boy next to her for a clue as to what to say. He started speaking.

"Well, Father, who are these gay people? Can you point them out to me if I go to church?" He turned and smirked at the girl.

"That is an inappropriate thing to ask me, but I am sure you know that. The fact is if you attend Mass you have probably sat by someone who is gay. So do you or your friend care to rethink your earlier statements?" I was being pretty tough on them now.

It was as much for their benefit to call them out on their misbehavior as it was to show the rest of the class how to stand up to such nonsense.

They were on their heels now. It was time to finish with them and move on. “There are plenty of lies spread about the Catholic Church. It is okay to stand up for what is true when you hear someone spreading falsehoods. That is not to say you should get into an argument with anyone. Speak the truth as Jesus did and be done.”

I turned my attention to the whole class. After the last back and forth their eyes and ears were upon me. Kids are interested in “what’s in it for me,” so I decided to address that thought.

“It is interesting that the people I know who are most joyous and content are those who practice their faith regularly. There has been research that indicates that people who are regular church goers and pray regularly are better able to handle the tough times that come in life."

This sweeping statement was met with silence. I glanced quickly at the two in the back row. They sat quietly staring at the floor. Time was running out, so I repeated that I would take another question. A girl in the front row meekly raised her hand.

"Were you going to talk about why girls can't be priests?" she asked.

"Thank you for reminding me. The Catholic Church would love to have women as priests. We cannot though because we follow the example of Jesus and he only made men priests. It seems obvious he had the idea to put men in the role of servant to the people as priests and women in a different role."

The girl's eyes grew as wide as I had ever seen anyone's eyes grow. "I never thought of it like that. So men who become priests are really our servants?" she asked with great excitement.

"That is correct."

She smiled at my answer. "I don't want to be anyone's servant. Now I am glad that men have to be priests."

The class laughed at this comment.

"Well", she said, "that means men are our servants. I think that is cool."

"It is not a bad thing to be a servant. Jesus acted as servant to everyone around him. Do you remember the Bible reading about him washing the feet of the Apostles?"

At this point silence again enveloped the class, but the kids really seemed to be thinking about what I had said. The wheels were really turning in some of their heads. It was best to leave on a positive note. I thanked Mr. Bois for the time with his class and I blessed all the students in the class. Always in my prayers, I would say an extra decade of the Rosary for them tonight.

It had been a long day. As I walked to my house I saw Mom's window was dark. She had always been an early riser. Carl was relaxing in the living room with a book and a glass of wine. I sat down across from him and silently thanked God for a good experience that evening. Carl looked up from his book.

"Everything go okay tonight with the classes, John?" he wondered.

"Yes quite well. I feel comfortable with the future of the church and especially this parish after spending time with the kids. There are some really good ones."

“Hmmm, that is good to hear. I was thinking of you tonight for some reason. I am glad it went well.”

“Maybe your ears were burning,” I mused. “They know you are living here and asked about you. It seemed to intrigue them that a Lutheran would be living in this house.”

“I suppose you told them that since I was in the wrong religion, I was going straight to hell.”

“Of course. You wouldn’t want me to lie to them, would you?”

“Funny thing is I had the same conversation with the kids at my church,” Carl puzzled out loud.

“Well,” I concluded, “only one of us can be right. And we both know who that is.”

“Glad we agree on something,” Carl seemed to agree.

The two of us relaxed and read for another hour before heading to bed.

CHAPTER ELEVEN

Things sometimes have an odd way of tying together.

The local women's shelter had provided comfort and safety for more than twenty years. It was the only such shelter in all of Nicollet County. Thankfully, throughout the years the six-bedroom house was always big enough to house every woman in need. Lately, that seemed to be changing. I received a call from the shelter manager saying that they were having to double up on some rooms because the number of women seeking refuge had steadily increased over the last few months. She told me that the average number of residents, usually four, had expanded to eight. This meant a need for more bedding materials, clothing and food. It also meant that more often a resident would be Catholic and my services were needed. When I received the call, I put away the paperwork I was working on and headed to the shelter.

Typically, whenever I traveled to console someone, I listened to a special kind of music. This would be a trip for consoling. I was told a woman of the Catholic faith had just moved into the shelter to escape an abusive husband. She had asked for a priest. The shelter manager told me the woman came from Minneapolis, hoping putting some distance between her and her spouse would keep her safe. I placed a CD of Gregorian Chants into my player. Somehow this beautiful sound set up my heart to be as compassionate as possible.

Arriving at the shelter, I noticed rain clouds moving in. A brisk wind swept into my face as I climbed out of my car. After a brief discussion with the shelter manager, I was introduced to the new resident. We walked to a private area referred to as an interview room and sat down.

The woman thanked me for coming. I encouraged her to take her time and tell me as much about her situation as she felt comfortable sharing. She told me nothing I had not heard many times before. Her dating relationship started off well. Her husband-to-be was charming and witty. He was a lot of fun to be around. After several months he proposed and she accepted. Then gradually things started changing. He became moody and grumpy. Sometimes he would be angry with her and accuse her of any number of things. She told herself it was because he was having problems at work and was stressed by the upcoming marriage. The woman convinced herself that after the wedding he would return to the happy person he had once been. He did not.

There would be days when she would come home from work and sit in her car. She would not be able to face walking in the front door because her husband would run up to her and yell at her for some imperceptible slight. She hoped it would get better but it got worse. The emotional toll was too much. She went to a friend's house but he followed her there and insisted on coming in. The police were called but they could not do much. So she left the city and came here.

The woman went through a lot of tissues as she told me this story. What she needed most was a compassionate ear, and that is what I gave her. This was not the time nor place for lectures or ideas as to how she should live her life. It was difficult for a person like me to remain quiet when seeing flaws in someone's thinking. I thank God for the ability to train myself to keep quiet and let people process their thoughts and feelings.

After ninety minutes she composed herself. I asked her if she would like to pray together and she replied she would. We prayed for twenty minutes, and I gave her my telephone number. I told her to contact me for any reason at any time of the day. She appeared very grateful. I left the interview room and walked to the front of the house. It was clear to me I would not be able to make it home without first going to the bathroom. Again, it is odd how things come together sometimes. Had I not paused for a trip to relieve myself, the following would not have happened. I walked back into the front room and saw a woman attempting to carry some packages into the house. She looked like some assistance would be welcome.

“Excuse me,” I said to her. The woman, fortyish, of average height and appearance save for some very red hair, seemed startled by me. I expect she was surprised to see a man in the house. Then she noticed my collar and was at ease.

“Oh, Father! You surprised me,” she laughed.

I immediately sized her up as a cheerful, upbeat lady. As we spoke, her manner proved to be delightful.

“I am sorry, I just saw you struggling and thought you might need some help,” I offered.

“Oh, if you don’t mind, sure. I have some more bags in the car.” With that, she set down her packages and strolled out to her minivan.

"You don't look much like a delivery person," I quipped.

"Thank you, I think." She smiled at me. "I volunteer here. I work part-time at a used clothing and dry goods store. Whenever there is a need for bedding and clothing and such, they call and I buy what I can and bring it down here. Lately, they have been receiving new residents at all hours of the day. It doesn't matter to me because my husband is very busy at his job and works long hours some weeks.

We don't have any children, so there is no reason I can't help out when needed."

"I must say that is very generous of you. So, if you do not mind my asking, do you pay for these items yourself?"

"It is not a big deal. My husband makes a good salary and the money I get working part-time is extra. I get some real good deals, too. When I first started doing this I told Suzie, the shelter manager, to call whenever someone arrived here. I should have known that, it being a shelter, people arrived at all hours of the evening. I'm not complaining, really. I love being a part of something that helps women in trouble."

Her enthusiasm was uplifting. She was the kind of person that you loved to be around. I carried in the last box of clothing and set it down on the reception counter. I turned to her as she followed me to the counter, her back straining to carry the big box she held. She smiled at me. I realized I had missed something important.

"Excuse me. I didn't get your name," I sheepishly admitted.

"Oh, I am sorry, Father Krentz." She had the better of me.

"You know me? You're not a parishioner, are you?" I hoped I hadn't embarrassed myself by not knowing one of my own.

"No, I'm a Methodist. I just recognize you because you're the parish priest. You know, Blessing is not that big of a town. You know who all the important people are - like ministers and doctors and such." She smiled at my blushing at being called important. She seemed to think it would make me more comfortable to find some linkage between us. "I think one of my neighbors is Catholic, though I don't know her that well. She seldom comes out of the house."

I got her back on track. "Your name?"

"Janie Mahoney," she finally told me.

"And we haven't met? I just ask because your name is familiar for some reason."

Janie curled her lip and furrowed her brow while she thought. "Nope," she affirmed, "I think I would remember if we had met before. I am glad we did now, though."

A lightning bolt of thought entered my slow-moving brain. The reason I was familiar with Janie's name was because my parishioner, Mrs. Kathy Johnson, had been gossiping about her with nasty accusations. Janie's bright, fun manner was on the opposite end of the spectrum of the person who strove so hard to destroy her reputation.

One of the truths about spending time with energetic, sweet-hearted people is that you are in no hurry to depart from their company. I spent another enjoyable ten minutes talking with Janie. I was impressed with everything about her. I was more than a little envious of the Methodist minister. Having someone like this in your church family would be a positive influence. As much as I enjoyed spending time with someone so upbeat, I couldn't bear to take up any more of her time. I told her how much I enjoyed meeting her and thanked her for her contribution to the shelter.

On the way home the sun came out and its warm rays felt like heaven on my face. I switched off my CD of chants and turned on the local AM Polka station.   The sounds were different but both were joyful. The drive home was too short.

CHAPTER TWELVE

The third Wednesday evening of every month was set aside for our Pastoral Council meeting. I can't think of anything more important than involving laymen with every possible aspect of the church. It is what Vatican II wanted, and it is what I embrace. The worst possible thing for a priest to do is wave an autocratic scepter over anything and everything connected with the parish. The members of the church fund it; they should have their say in how it runs.

Frankly, most of the best ideas that we have implemented in this church did not originate with me. I see my role as being one of overall management and guidance, working with a talented, smart group of council members.

We have not always agreed on everything, and when the matters have crept into the realm of liturgical issues, I have had the final say, of course. It has been my hope that the council would agree that I have always treated them and their opinions with respect. Doing any less would be short-sighted on my part.

This night we had a number of issues to discuss. There were the usual minor housekeeping chores but also some major decisions to be made. One of the most important agenda items was the need to appoint a new Chairperson. I was a little uncomfortable with the discussion about this matter at the last meeting. Our current chair dropped several hints that he wanted to continue in the role, although the charter expressly prohibited it. The purpose of the prohibition against repeating a term as chair was to keep anyone from establishing themselves as an indispensable person. It would not do to allow someone to build themselves a personal fiefdom. Worse, the person would be seen as my right hand man and as having influence and power. Still worse, what if I got so used to dealing with this person that I ignored everyone else's right to speak up and have some effect on the church? Violating the charter would tell others in the parish that there was a chosen person – the beginning of a clique. It would tell the other folks they were not as important to the church or the priest. It would contribute to the downfall and demise of the church.

I got to the meeting a few minutes early. It looked like a full house. Kurt O'Hara, our chair, was present, as was Cathy Daneeli, the vice-chair. Kurt always tried his best to provide some leadership to the council. He had thick, flowing red hair that always made him stand out from anyone around. When he would get excited his cheeks would light up with red to match his hair. Overall, he had done a fine job during his term, though sometimes I worried that he took himself too seriously. This was just a regular church in a small town and he was the Pastoral Council Chair. Sometimes he appeared to think he was the CEO of a large corporation. A priest always worries that a small amount of authority will go to someone's head. The worst thing that can happen in any church is for one person to be singled out as special to the priest. The impression that gives people is that they are not as important as the priest's favorite. The inevitable result is people start falling away from the church. That was not going to happen under my watch.

The other members of the council appeared ready to do some business. Kurt called the meeting to order. The first order of business was reading and approving the last meeting minutes. Standard order of businesses were quickly taken care of. We moved on to the main topic.

"Well," Kurt began, "we need to appoint a chair for the next two-year term. I know a lot of you don't have much interest and are busy with your personal lives. It is true that I have experience at this post that the rest of you don't."

The faces around the table ranged from disinterest to shock to humiliation. I sighed.

"It's a big job," Kurt emphasized. "I am willing to throw my hat in the ring for another two-year term. That way we will have continuity."

"Continuity?" I exclaimed. That was as lame of a reason as there could be.

"Well, Father, we are considering a capital project to fix the roof. It would be best to have me stay in this role while we do it. Besides, I know the president of a firm who would help us solicit funds from the parishioners. They do that kind of thing."

"Yes," I said, "that firm manages capital campaigns for churches throughout the state. They also charge tens of thousands of dollars for the service. Their cost estimate for taking charge of the capital campaign equaled two months' worth of collections. What would the parishioners say about that?"

"We don't have to tell anyone." Kurt came up with a solution which, if accepted, would be such a scandal it would close the church.

"Transparency," I stated forcefully, "is how this church is run. We don't get our way by hiding things from the people who donate their hard-earned money to pay for things."

Kurt had not yet accepted that I had built a brick wall in front of him.

"Father, the fact is there are a lot of older couples in this parish. Their kids are grown and they have savings set aside. We could tap into that and have ample funds – not just for the roof but for all sorts of projects. There's no limit to the number of things we can build. New rooms for these meetings, for instance. And a new youth room." His excitement was getting the best of him.

The picture Kurt was painted sounded familiar. I wondered if Mrs. Satane had been spending time with him. Neither she nor he seemed to understand the fact that the basement of the church was well furnished with classrooms for the kids and two meeting rooms for meetings. He was so caught up in his fantasy that it was going to take some doing to bring him back down to earth. The best time to start was now.

"Kurt, why do we need new rooms? The rooms we have now are adequate. Our parish has actually shrunk in size." A dose of reality was my first attempt at reason.

"Well, maybe if we build new rooms alongside the church, more people will move into the parish," Kurt said eagerly.

"Why would anyone move to this parish from another city because we built a new classroom or meeting room?"

“Because, you know . . . ” This poorly thought through blurb was the best he could do.

“People will sell their homes and move to Blessing because we built a new room?”

“We don’t know if we don’t try.” Kurt actually seemed to think he was being convincing. “We can tell our current parishioners it will work. Enough of them will go along with it so we can get the money we need.”

“And Kurt, you’re okay with taking people’s savings – under false pretenses? Or delaying their retirement so we can build a monument to ourselves?” The other council members were squirming in their seats. This was getting unpleasant.

“A monument to you, Father. We’ll add to the church with a new room and name it after you.”

I buried my head in my hands. That Kurt did not realize how asinine his statement was could only be outweighed by the fact that he thought I would be thrilled to see my name on this boondoggle.

"Of course," Kurt added, "we could always put my name in letters on the plaque somewhere too. Smaller letters than your name, of course." Kurt forced a false humble smile.

"We are not engaging in establishing a legacy for me or anyone else by spending other people's money. Especially under less than honest pretenses. Under no circumstances. Never." I used my most serious tone of voice. Kurt's expression changed. He looked like a sixteen-year-old whose dad had just poked holes in his story about getting an "F" on his report card because the dog ate his homework. This entire matter reinforced my belief that we needed a new Pastoral Council Chair. The small amount of power and status Kurt felt had swelled his head beyond my comprehension.

"Kurt, we are done with this discussion. If the parish ever does grow again we will discuss a building project. And if that does happen, under no circumstances will my name be associated with it. The last thing any priest should do is focus on himself. Are we clear?" I said this as gently as I could, but am sure I came across strong.

"Okay, Father," was all he could answer.

"Please solicit nominations from the council now for the new chair," I requested. It was not normally my place to move things along, but this was a special situation.

Kurt looked stunned. I realized he thought even after this discussion he would remain as chair. I did not want an ugly situation. When someone is flustered it is difficult to know what they will do next. It was not my role to lead the meeting and I had no intention of doing so. I needed him to step up.

Leaning over to him, I whispered, “Kurt, please.”

Kurt pretended not to hear me. His face flushed with anger. At last he started to speak.

“Well, Father wants someone to replace me. Who thinks they can handle this job? I will warn you, it is a lot of work with no thanks whatsoever.” His mouth formed a ghoulish scowl.

That cold statement had the intended consequences of silencing the council. The council members stared down at the table. The seconds ticked past. This was spinning out of control. I would have to get involved.

“Historically,” I began, “the outgoing chair helps out the incoming chair with the details. I, of course, am also available to help the new person get their feet wet. Didn’t Kari Caster help you, Kurt, when she was the outgoing chair?”

Kurt took a long time to reply. Perhaps he was trying to think of a way to deny what I said. Maybe he did not want to spend next Saturday in confession relating a lie. Whatever his thought process, he finally spewed something out.

"Yes, Kari did help. She was actually very helpful to me."

"I am certain that you will carry on the tradition Kari began. Maybe you even want to write down some procedures and hints. You could author a manual that would be the standard for future chairs." I was laying it on pretty thick.

"Author?" Kurt embraced the word.

"Author is a word reserved for people with time and talent. I think you are one of those people." I was rolling. I was determined to somehow make a win out of this for Kurt. Everyone let their ego run away with them from time to time. He was only being human. Serving the council for as long as he did was a fine contribution and deserved some recognition.

"Father," Candy Ringer, one of the council members, spoke up, "I would be interested in serving as Pastoral Council Chair. If you think I could do it."

"Thank you for your interest, Candy, but you are addressing the wrong person. It is Kurt's role to provide information about the position and take nominations."

"Thank you, Father." Kurt was back in the game. He was reinvigorated. After ten minutes of discussing the tasks involved with being the chair Kurt bent over backwards coming up with ways he would help with the transition. The council took a vote and unanimously elected Candy as the new chair. During this time I folded my hands and sat quietly.

As the meeting drew to a close I asked Kurt if I could say something. I pulled out a card that I had all the members sign after Mass last weekend. It was a "thank-you" card for Kurt's service. There was a gift card at a local restaurant that I paid for out of my own pocket. I told Kurt it was a small token of all of the council and the parish's appreciation. It looked like tears were going to start coming so I said the closing prayer. Kurt gaveled the meeting to a close and everyone got up to leave.

I congratulated Candy as we walked out the door together. I did not know her very well, but she seemed eager to learn and was dedicated. I knew it would work out fine.

CHAPTER THIRTEEN

A priest is on call seven days a week. I always tried to keep Wednesday afternoons open to give myself some free time I could rely on. As much as I loved my profession, it was important to my mental health to recharge every week. This worked well for years. There would be the occasional emergency of course where I had to rush to the hospital because someone fell ill, but I found I could depend on this time off every week.

After Carl moved in, I found that he too had Wednesday afternoons off. At first I was concerned that we would be tripping over each other, but as it turned out he loved spending time outdoors, so we seldom saw each other during these mid-week breaks. He loved all things athletic – golfing, biking, jogging – you name it and he did it.

It was one of the more pleasant days of the summer. I had placed my lounge chair out in the backyard and had gone back into the house to locate a book. I was undecided between taking my book about the Revolutionary War or a new detective story from my favorite Minnesota author. I decided to take both books and alternate chapters. Such was the good life of man with nothing to do on a lazy summer day.

Carl walked into the house as I was leaving it. He looked as if a thought came into his head when he saw me. I kept walking and he followed me out to my chair.

"Hi, Carl. What are your plans for this wonderful day?"

"Well, John, I was going to drive down to the river and run a few miles."

"Sounds like a good plan, Carl. Enjoy." I opened my book. Carl continued standing by me. I looked up at him. "Problem, Carl?"

"One of my flock just called me on my cell phone."

"Oh, no. An emergency?" If it was, I couldn't imagine why he was just standing around, talking to me.

"No, far from it. This man, his name is Roscoe. He and his wife are members of the Valley Country Club."

"Oh, sure. I have never been there but it is supposed to be very nice. It is exclusive, members only, right?"

"Yes, I have played there as a guest of a member from time to time. It is the best place I have ever played. The greens are immaculate. The rough is better than the public course fairway."

"I'm not sure what that means, but I guess it is good."

"You ever play golf, John?" Carl asked in a suspicious sort of way. I began to get wary.

"I have played a few times. Enough to know I am no good at it. I guess the last time was a few years ago. I think I am what you call a duffer."

"John, Roscoe and his wife have a standing reservation at Valley every Wednesday afternoon. He just told me something came up and they would not be able to use their reservation. He just gave me the reservations. No expense to me and my partner at all. It's all free. This is a great opportunity."

"Quite a break for you." I smiled. I then stared at Carl, waiting for him to lead the conversation to a conclusion.

"The thing is, they set us up in foursomes. There will be two other players there, and I need someone to come with me."

I now realized why Carl was talking with me. He had to be desperate to come to me. A good friend, which I considered myself to be, would jump at the chance to help out.

"I wish I could help, but my afternoon is pretty well set."

"John, you know how you tell your parishioners all the time that they should try new things."

"How do you know what I tell parishioners? Have you been sneaking into Mass?" It was obvious my day was spinning out of control so I had to get some fun out of the situation before succumbing.

"And you know," Carl said, ignoring my question, "how you preach that one should always help out a friend?"

"I hope I don't take as long to get to the point as you are now."

"You know, John, the fresh air would be great for you. A little exercise, too. Such a beautiful day to be outside."

"Carl, I am outside. And you know what Mark Twain said about golf. A good walk ruined."

"Ha, ha. You got me there, John. You know what – if we leave now we have time for a quick lesson with the golf pro. I'll even pay for it."

"You will open up that moth-eaten pocketbook of yours? I guess it would be worth losing my day off to see that."

"I saw a bag of clubs when John Paul was cleaning out the garage. Those must be yours?"

"Yeah, those are mine. Some parishioner thought my life was too carefree so he gave me a gift some years back. I have not got much use out of them."

"I will get them and put them in the truck of my car. You better put some loose-fitting, comfortable clothes on. Hurry, we don't have much time."

Making as big a show of my anguish as I could, I picked up my books and headed into the house. Mom seemed surprised and maybe a tad amused when I told her of my change in plans for the day. She told me she been interested in my detective book and asked to borrow it.

As we pulled out of the driveway I felt the sin of envy enter me as I watched mom walk out to my lounge chair with my book in her hand. Oh, well.

It was a glorious day for a drive. No one wants a pouty priest, so I checked my self-pity and resolved to enjoy the day. The sun shone brightly and I embraced the day God granted to me.

As we pulled up into the drive at the club I noticed most of the cars were new and expensive makes. This really was not my natural habitat. Men and women were dressed in fancy clothes. I looked down at the old pair of jeans I was wearing. My polo shirt was clean enough, thanks to mom's good work, but was older than every car we passed. The humility felt good.

We checked in at the desk, and Carl arranged for a quick lesson for me. The pro, a young woman, sized me up rather quickly. It was clear to her I was not an avid golfer and did not have the ability to become more than a below average hacker. She taught me a few basics, just enough to keep me from completely embarrassing myself on the links.

After fifteen minutes of intense work, she let me hit a few balls on the driving range. Surprising myself, I did much better than I had ever done. Of ten balls, I shanked two, sliced four and had four short but relatively straight drives. I was ready to take on all comers.

Carl tried to look cheerful, though I am sure he was having second thoughts about bringing me out there. I did not want him to feel bad so acted as cheerful as I could. My main concern was that I not embarrass him in front of other golfers.

“Carl, I am ready to take on the world,” I declared, full of vim and vigor.

“Glad to hear it, John. You did have some nice drives there.” He tried to be encouraging.

“One favor – if I do anything inappropriate, you will let me know, won’t you?”

“I wouldn’t worry about that, John. There’s not much you can really do out here that is not appropriate,” he reassured me.

"So," I asked, "if I pick up my ball and carry it from the tee to the green?"

"Maybe that. But only if we are betting money."

"Sounds fair enough to me."

We got our golf cart and headed to the first tee. There were two men there waiting. They would fill out our foursome. I never understood the requirement for having four people play together, but then again I didn't understand many things about golf. They were very well dressed. I thought they might be bankers or doctors. I was sure they were not members of my parish. We walked over and introduced ourselves.

"Hello," Carl said to the two men, "my name is Carl and this is John. We'll be rounding out your foursome today."

The men studied us and seemed to come to the conclusion that we were neither bankers nor doctors. They were friendly.

“Good to meet you, Carl and John. My name is Thomas and this is Winston.”

We shook hands and exchanged pleasantries about the weather and the shape of the course.

Thomas insisted Carl and I tee up first, so I pulled my driver out of the bag and reached into the pocket for a ball. I had none. I turned to Carl but he was teeing up his ball. As little as I knew about the game, I knew to keep quiet when someone is about to hit the ball. I was getting a little nervous. It didn’t matter to me personally, but I did not want to embarrass Carl by admitting I couldn’t play.

Winston leaned over to me and whispered, "Did you know you have to careful on the layup to the third green? There's a new bunker."

I quietly thanked him and turned to watch Carl hit a fine drive into the middle of the fairway. Whatever Winston just told me was probably important, although it made no sense whatever. Why I would want to lay on the third green was a mystery to me.

As Carl walked back to the cart I intercepted him. "Carl, do you have a spare ball?" I asked.

At first Carl did not seem to understand why I was asking this question. Then the shock of how ill-prepared his partner was registered, and he opened up a pocket on his golf bag. He grabbed two balls out of his bag and handed them to me. I could not imagine why he would give me two balls when you can only hit one but soon found out.

Winston and Thomas were busy whispering to each other. I am sure the subject of their conversation was me. I teed the ball and took the mightiest swing I could. The ball sailed to within ten feet of the green. I was pretty happy until I noticed the flag on the green my ball lay near had a number "9" on it.

"Remember what the pro said about slicing the ball," Carl gently reminded me.

"I will hit the next one straight," I assured him. And I did. I powered the ball right down the middle of the fairway. I was proud of my shot until I realized the ball landed about one hundred years short of Carl's drive. I walked back to the cart and watched as both Winston and Thomas smacked their drives well past the distance of Carl's and my combined shots. It was going to be a long day.

After struggling through the first three holes, we had time for a break. There was a foursome in front of us that was moving slow.

This was a blessing for me, as it gave me a chance to calm down and figure out how to get through the rest of the game. A few peaceful minutes did a great deal for me when I was stressed out. Unfortunately, my peace was cut short. Winston and Thomas had lit up cigars and strolled over to where I was sitting with Carl.

"So," Winston drawled, "you fellas married? That's why we come out to the course, to get away from the wives." He laughed.

"No," Carl quickly replied, wanting to put a lid on the topic as soon as possible.

"I get it," Thomas said, although he didn't. "you two play the field, huh? I bet you thrill all the ladies in town, if you know what I mean."

Neither Winston nor Thomas appeared able to see the clear visual cue Carl was providing. His head was turned away from them, and he appeared uninterested in their topic of conversation.

During our discussions it was obvious Carl would always grieve his beloved wife. He was here today to enjoy the sun and play some golf, not to engage in banter about dating. I decided I had better step in.

"Actually, guys we are off the market. I am a priest. Carl is a Lutheran minister."

They both laughed. Still not getting it, Winston spoke further. "Yeah, we're both priests, too. Ha, ha. My favorite part of church is when I take up the collection. That's how I pay for all my beer." He and Thomas both laughed uproariously at what they thought was a clever joke. Carl and I sat expressionless. They studied our expressions and were puzzled as to why we were so serious. A light bulb must have gone on in Winston's head.

"You mean you both really are priests?" he asked.

"I am a priest. Carl is a Lutheran minister. Neither of us is married. So, are you two married?" I tried to turn the conversation around to them, hoping it would smooth things out.

"Married? Yeah, we're both married. Between us we've had five wives. Ain't that a hoot?" Winston said, as he winked at Thomas.

"We love being married so much that we keep doing it," Thomas declared. The two smiled at each other.

Winston declared, "We can't say anything bad about divorce, though. The fact is it has been good, real good to us." Thomas nodded his approval.

I had been watching the foursome ahead of us to see if it would be safe to hit our drives and move down the fairway and away from this conversation. What Winston just said had me curious, so I did the unthinkable. I asked him to explain.

"What do I mean?" Winston repeated my question. "I guess we did not mention we are lawyers. Divorce lawyers. We specialize in divorce. About fifteen years ago we stumbled across each other while representing dueling spouses. We formed our own little law firm, and it's been fat city ever since then. You won't see us driving two-year-old cars. We buy new every year." Winston smiled proudly.

Thomas joined in. "And we have two of the finest houses in Blessing. Actually," a broad smile came to his lips, "we've owned several of the finest houses in Blessing."

"Now our exes own some of the finest houses," Winston laughed. "That's okay, though, we don't mind taking care of them. We of course had them sign pre-nups, so they got a place to live and that was about all."

"Children?" Carl asked, as curious as I had become about these two.

"We each have children with our ex-wives," Winston explained. "I have three total. One with the first wife and two with the second. Or is it two with the first and three with the second?" He laughed. "I get confused sometimes."

"I have three kids with the first wife," Thomas said. "I, well, I guess we both did the same thing with our current wives. We said no kids or no marriage. Kids just aren't a part of our lives. Our wives got it, which is good or they'd get the boot."

"Wow," was all I could say.

"Do you get to see your kids?" Carl wondered.

"Not so much. We're both busy. And our new wives don't much care for them. That's okay, neither one of us is much for dirty diapers anyway."

"Winston," Carl asked, "how old are your kids?"

Winston thought for a few seconds. "They're both teenagers. One is fifteen and I think the girl is thirteen. Or something like that."

"So they are well past the diaper stage. And the third child? You said you had three?" Carl attempted to get the full story.

"Oh yeah, him. I guess he is ten now. I don't know. His mom remarried and they moved out of state."

Carl and I sadly looked at each other. As depressing as it was to listen, it was important that we understood these men. Their personal stories, a more accurate term would be tragedies, reflected much of the state of society. Children without fathers grew up with two strikes against them. Carl and I exchanged knowing glances. There was no need to exchange words. We were on the same wavelength. We both knew what we had to do. I make a habit of telling my parishioners to be open to God's guidance. Opportunities abound, but we are so often caught up with our own needs or wallowing in self-pity that we miss the chance to do what God wants us to do. I wasn't going to miss out on a chance to help these two men. Whether they knew it or not, they were missing out an important part of their lives – their children. Folks like this usually put their shame and their troubles in a deep, dark place at the bottom of the heart. They denied the pain and the guilt that came with ignoring the needs of their own flesh and blood. The result was they continued to seek meaning and happiness while they drove away from it as fast as they could.

Carl and I approached Winston and Thomas as one. "Hey, guys. We are both thinking that we should change the teams."

They both looked at us oddly. We would need to be clearer. Sneaky, but clear.

"Honestly," and I was being honest, "I don't know anything about this game. Carl is much more adept at the sport but we would both benefit from your sharing your wisdom. Perhaps I should ride in the cart with you, Winston. Carl and Thomas can team up. That would give us time to get acquainted while you teach me how to strike a ball straight."

"How about it, Thomas?" Winston asked. "I guess experts like us owe it to these two priests to help them somewhat."

"He's a priest, I'm a minister," Carl corrected Winston. He bit his lip after that, realizing what we intended to do could not be done by lecture.

During my first turn as a priest I was assigned as an associate someone I will refer to as Fr. Starn, a good and holy man. I always suspected the purpose of my association was to instruct me how not to win people over. Whenever someone approached Fr. Starn with an issue, he would strictly lecture them. Such a lack of compassion turned people off. It seemed as if every week fewer people attended Mass. His response to the weak turnout was to stand at the pulpit and harangue those who did show up.

Even a fool such as myself knew that if I muttered one word of criticism to Winston, he would tune me out and my attempt at intervention would be finished. This was not the time to suggest he begin to take the role of parent on nor was it the time to be anything but quiet. I would listen.

For the next couple of holes Winston drove the cart with his foot firmly pressed on the accelerator. He seemed uncomfortable with me as his partner. I suspect he suspected my true purpose. I broke the silence by talking about what seemed to be his favorite subject – himself. We finished the front nine and I had a good history of Winston's college days and his career. He never once mentioned his wife, ex-wives, or kids.

As it turned out, Winston did know a few things about golf. He was able to help me with my game more than the pro I spent time with earlier. I made sure to thank him repeatedly.

By the sixteenth hole it seemed Winston was feeling comfortable with me. I kept an eye on Carl and Thomas. They seemed to be hitting it off pretty well. Carl was far more extroverted than me and had a wonderful way of developing relationships. Earlier in our friendship I would have felt a competition but thankfully had grown to the state where I was now rooting for his success.

At the seventeenth hole we hit our drives and took a minute to enjoy the bright sunshine and clean air hitting our lungs. Carl and Thomas mounted up and rode off to chase their drives. Winston stood just staring at the fairway as I slid my driver into my golf bag. You don't make it in my profession unless you can read people. Winston was a book that had been locked shut, but now the cover had been flipped open. We played the entire hole without either of us saying a word. My main concern was that we were about to run out of time. When I first set foot on the golf course, eighteen holes seemed like an eternity in perdition. I wanted it over as quickly as possible. Now I wished we could play another dozen.

As we teed up for the final hole, Carl and Thomas stood quietly talking. Winston had hit only powerful drives throughout the game. This time he shanked the ball. It flew a fraction of the usual distance and hit a tree in the rough. Something was messing with his mind.

Winston put together a couple spectacular shots and his ball rolled on the green a few feet from the hole. In one minute he would be back with Thomas and his natural instinct of hiding his emotions would come back into being.

"Winston. Would you do me a favor?" I politely asked.

"Sure, Johnny. Anything." He was equally polite in responding. The usual bluster he spewed out was absent. There was a marked change in his mannerism.

This was my only chance. Probably not a good chance but a chance. I put my hand into my pocket and pulled out my wallet. Winston's eyes grew wide.

"John, we did not bet anything on this game. The truth is, Thomas and I usually take the people we play with for a few bucks but you being who you are and all, we didn't think it right. Besides," his bluster came back for a minute, "you are the worst golfer I ever played with. It would be like stealing to bet with you."

I chuckled. Winston was funny. I am sure most people enjoyed his company. But deep down he was experiencing an emptiness that I could do nothing about. I could guide him to someone who could. I pulled my business card out of my wallet and handed it to him.

"Would you call me sometime, Winston? Just to talk. I would like to know how you are doing. You are busy, I know, but I would like to hear how things are going. My office is open all the time to you, too. You should feel free to stop by anytime."

"Father, I mean, John. I am not Catholic. I haven't even been inside a church since my first marriage."

"It's my business," I softly informed Winston. "It is what I do. Your choice of religion is not important to me. *You* are what is important to me."

Winston nodded and walked up to the green. With all the confidence and ability of a professional golfer, he sunk his ball with one stroke. It took me four tries to get my ball in that lousy little cup. As Carl pulled out four balls from that miserable round hole in the ground we smiled and shook hands. The four of us walked back to the clubhouse. There was no talking, only the measured pacing of our footsteps. Thomas was the first to speak as we arrived at the door.

"Looks like Winston and I should buy the first round here today for our new buddies. What do you say, guys? Let's grease up the gills a little bit with some bad liquor."

Carl spoke for me as a brother-in-arms could. "We are not big drinkers, and the fact is we each have work waiting for us at home. I really enjoyed meeting the both of you, and we thank you for putting up with our attempt at the game of golf. And Thomas, remember what I said."

Thomas nodded and he and Winston disappeared into the clubhouse. Carl and I turned and headed for the car. We were halfway there when I heard my name called.

“Father John!”

After spending four hours with Winston, I immediately recognized his voice. I spun around and saw him walking quickly towards me.

“Carl, I will meet up with you at the car.”

“Right, John. No rush. Take your time.” And he headed away. “John,” Winston again spoke my name as he walked up to me, “thank you.”

“For what, exactly?” I smiled. “There is nothing to thank me for.”

“For listening to me. No one ever listens to me.”

This seemed odd, given Winston’s propensity to talk nonstop. He was engaging and funny. I then realized he was talking about something deeper.

"I tell jokes and kid around but no one ever cares about me. No one cares about what is going on inside me. Thomas is a great guy, but when I've tried to talk about things that really matter, like my marriage and kids and things, he gets uncomfortable and changes the subject. I can't even talk with my wife. Never could talk with any of them. No one really wants to hear what is going on with me."

"Well, I do. And I apologize for just giving you my card and telling you to call me. Let's set up an appointment. You can stop by whenever it is convenient for you. How about on your way to or from work?"

Winston thought for a moment. "Is it okay if I do that and keep it between you and me? I don't want to keep anything from my wife, but you know how it is."

“Well, for now let’s just meet for coffee Tuesday morning. Once you feel more comfortable, you should explain to your wife that we are getting together – just two friends talking.”

“Thanks, John. You know, I have been worried for a long time that I was going to wind up having to see a shrink. But you give me hope I don’t need to.”

“There was a Bishop once who said that a lot of people who think they need mental health help just need to admit they have a need for God in their lives. Maybe you are one of those people.”

Winston shook his head. “But you know I am not converting, right?”

“We are two friends getting together every week for coffee. I am looking forward to it. I will see you next Tuesday at 7:00 a.m.”

Winston nodded and half turned to walk away. Then he stopped and walked up and threw his arms around me. He gave me a bear hug. Winston let go and without saying a word walked back up the clubhouse. He almost got to the door when Thomas came out.

"Winston, how long does it take to walk out to your car and get your wallet? The beer is getting warm."

"Don't drink it all up, you rotten bum," Winston hollered, trying to appear like he had not a care in the world. Then he laughed.

I climbed into Carl's car. The burden so many folks silently carry with them never ceased to astonish me. I thanked God that I had an opportunity to provide some degree of comfort to one of his children.

"Thank you for coming with today, John. I always enjoy your company and a round of golf. But today was special. I think we both had a chance to touch some lives today. That is what we do, isn't it?"

"It is, Carl. It seems like rather than trying to drive, I should be a passenger."

"I'm not sure what you mean, John."

"Sometimes I wonder about all my plans to evangelize. Instead of seeking out opportunities, half of my mission can be accomplished by just being there for people as God guides them to us. How did things go with you?"

"I did have a nice chat with Thomas. I never talked directly about his kids of course. I just mused about my own family when I was growing up. Going fishing with my brother and dad. I spoke of all the memories I had. Just planting seeds, you know. Maybe something good will come out of it. I gave him my business card and told him to call me."

“Ha!” I exclaimed. “I did the same thing.”

“The first time one of my minister friends told me about having business cards I was stunned. I thought they were only for business people. Accountants and lawyers. I am glad I bought some. You never know when you will need one, but you are glad you have them when you do.”

“My Bishop, Bishop O’Reilly, suggested all priests get business cards. I did so reluctantly, but it is good I did. You see, he and I have a system worked out.”

“A system?” Carl wondered what I meant.

“Whenever he makes a suggestion, I find fault with it. Then I do it anyway because, after all, he is the boss. Then the suggestion works out great and I have to force myself to admit it to him.”

"How long have you two been married?" Carl asked.

That comment did not warrant even a slightly dirty look on my part. That is because I was not done giving my own version of confession.

"It was his idea to have Mom move into the house. I needed a housekeeper and my dad had just died."

"What a blessing to have her live with you. Evie is someone very special." There was no arguing with that.

"It is. Sometimes we have to remind each other I am not fifteen years old. I really don't know what I would do without her."

"Evie is a wonderful woman. It has improved my life knowing her. It can't be easy to have to cook and clean after someone who is so hard to get along with and so messy." Carl looked over to make sure I was paying attention. "But enough about what you're like to live with."

"A little clumsy, but an "A" for effort, Carl." It was a worthy try on his part; I had to give him some credit.

On the way home we had the sort of conversation only two good friends can have. We discussed sports, the weather, friends we have known, favorite music, anything and everything. Fortunately, I had brought my sunglasses; otherwise, the shine of the sun through the windshield would have been more than I could stand.

There was no way the day could get any better, or so I thought. Again proven wrong, to my delight we pulled into the driveway and discovered Mom had brought out the charcoal grill. She was making burgers soaked in an onion and garlic sauce of her own creation. Cold beers were brought out and the end of the day was celebrated as I think God intended – with joy and love.

CHAPTER TWELVE

If I have learned anything from my life it is that storms slide in on the tail end of golden rays of sunshine. People cannot be so enthralled by gilded beams of light that they forget to check the horizon for coming dark times. So even though I thoroughly enjoyed my previous day's golfing experience and supper with Carl and Mom, I couldn't not look over my shoulder. Perhaps there is a psychological sickness that describes my condition, but if there is, I don't care. It is a defense mechanism that keeps me from being caught flat-footed. I guess that means that deep down, rooted among my numerous other personality flaws, I am a control freak. And, I will now record, with good reason.

The day was busy as any but not overly so. I had a few appointments in the morning. First, an accountant from the company that takes care of our books stopped by. We went over the financials. There were no surprises. Times were tight as always, but we were in the black and doing as well as could be expected.

Next, I had back-to-back appointments with parishioners. Things went as well as I could expect.

Mom had some leftover salads from the previous evening's feast set up for lunch. Carl always carried his lunch to his office at his church, so we rarely saw him during the day. Mom would eat with me unless she was out with her friends or visiting my sisters in Wisconsin.

I had a one o'clock appointment, so was relaxing over the crumbs of my lunch. I took a sip of my lemonade and my attention was caught by a car door slamming. My appointment was here ten minutes early. This parishioner had a standing appointment at the same time every Thursday and was always punctual but never this early. I asked Mom if she would let the parishioner into my office while I made a quick trip to the bathroom. While there, I heard a second car door slam. Puzzled by this, I wondered if my appointment had forgotten something in her purse and needed to go back to the car. I walked out of the bathroom and through the kitchen and saw my appointment, who I will refer to as Mrs. Neese, making her way up the steps.

"Hello, Mrs. Neese, how are you today?" I asked.

"Hello, Father John. I am well," she calmly responded.

"Did you forget something in your car and have to go back to it?" It was none of my business, I was just curious about the door slamming twice a few minutes apart.

She was confused by my question. She did not seem to understand what I had asked. It did not seem worth pursuing, so I dropped the issue and invited her back to my office. As I led Mrs. Neece down the hallway, I saw Mom standing in my office doorway. She looked uncomfortable and a bit frazzled. I entered my office with Mrs. Neece immediately behind me. All my questions were answered by whom I saw.

"BISHOP O'REILLY!?" I expounded. There was nothing I expected less than to see the Bishop.

"Hello, John." He saw Mrs. Neece behind me and rephrased his greeting. "Hello, Father John."

"Johnny, I did not know what you would want me to do, so I brought His Eminence into your office." Mom apologetically explained.

"That is the right thing to do, Mom," I consoled her. She tried so hard to do the correct thing. Her role was not to be a receptionist and she had nothing to apologize for. No one would have known what to do in this instance. She had done well.

I introduced the Bishop to Mrs. Neece. She was as stunned as I was to see him sitting in my office. Mom quietly left the room to allow me to sort things out. The awkwardness of this situation could not easily be dealt with. I could not very well throw out my parishioner, but one does not ignore the Bishop.

"Bishop O'Reilly," I began to sort things out, "I did not expect you."

"I know, Father. There is an issue which came up that I did not want to handle over the phone. I was in Mankato at the time I heard of the issue and thought it best to stop in to discuss the matter with you on my way home. I do apologize for arriving with no notice. I was hoping to get here when you had space in your schedule."

"Mrs. Neece has a standing appointment at this time each week, Your Eminence."

Mrs. Neece obviously felt uncomfortable. This was the last thing I wanted. I was a parish priest because I wanted to minister to the people in my community. They were second only to God.

"I can leave, Father. I don't wish to be a problem," Mrs. Neece kindly said. This was the last thing I wanted. Members of my flock should never feel like they are problems.

"No," I begged, "please do not go. Bishop O'Reilly, can we please meet at another time? I will drive to your office tomorrow or even tonight if this is important."

The Bishop realized what a jam he had placed me in. Mrs. Neece slowly began to back out the door. The Bishop bit his lip. He was quite disappointed but understood it was a problem of his own doing. Happily, he did the right thing.

"Father, how many appointments do you have this afternoon?"

“After Mrs. Neece and I are done I have a space of one hour. Would that be enough time?”

“May I use your telephone in the next room to conduct some business for the next hour? I can get a lot done during that time.”

I asked Mrs. Neece to take a seat. Then I brought the Bishop out to the kitchen and placed the telephone on the table. Mom reappeared and made him a pot of tea. He seemed quite content, and I was relieved that he had not tried to assert himself by taking Mrs. Neece’s appointment time.

Mrs. Neece and I had our usual prayerful, productive meeting. Prompt as always, she glanced at her watch one minute before the hour ended and thanked me for my time. I walked her to the door and opened it for her. The Bishop stood and wished her well.

I asked the Bishop to accompany me back to my office. He politely thanked mom for her hospitality and we made our way to room. The Bishop sat down and immediately said, "A man walked into the kitchen while I was on the phone. He said hi to Evie as he made a beeline to the refrigerator. He mumbled 'Hi, man,' to me as he stuffed some food in his face and walked back outside."

"His name is John Paul."

"John Paul? Are you joking?"

"No. That is his name. He lives here."

"Lives here? In this house?"

"No, sir. He lives in the garage. Really. He has made a room for himself in the garage. He does some maintenance work around the house and yard. It is a long story."

"I thought you could not afford any more help?"

"We don't pay him. It's a room and board arrangement. I think of it as a "What would Jesus do" situation. One day I'm a parish priest; the next I run a home for wayward boys."

The Bishop was not pleased about this news. Any other time he would have taken me to task about it, but something else was on his mind. He was determined to share his burden with me.

"It's been quite a few months. I haven't heard anything from you, so I assume everything is going well with you and Reverend Carl," he said, testing the waters.

"We've had our moments, good and bad. I trust the additional income is benefitting the Diocese?"

"Yes, yes. Thank you for being so flexible and taking him in. I know you did not want to do so."

There's a reason they make certain men Bishops. Besides his learning and devotion to God he could also read people and understand circumstances. He doggedly went ahead with some unwelcome probing.

"Am I correct that things have worked out better than either of us imagined?" There was considerable hope in his voice as well as more than a glimmer of satisfaction.

My innate lack of tact was fed by my curiosity about what was going on. I rushed past the small talk.

"Yes, score one for the Bishop. Now, Kevin, why don't you share why you are here, today?"

A grim wave of expression flowed over his face. I braced myself. This wasn't going to be good.

"Well, we need to talk. We need to make some changes."

“Oh, no. I think we had this same discussion a few months ago.”

“And thank you for being open to it. The rumor is that you and Reverend Carl have become close friends.”

“It is funny how things work out. He is a holy man, but then compared to me most people look good. Now are you going to keep me in suspense any longer? The more you avoid talking about what you came here for, the worse I think it is going to be.”

“This isn’t easy, John. Well, you still have space in your house. At least one free bedroom in this house, if I am to understand that that man, John Paul, really does sleep in the garage.”

I was overcome with adrenaline. My legs straightened out. I stood up and threw my hands in the air.

“Kevin, this is not a hotel that you need to fill up!”

"Now, listen here, John."

"What religion will be represented this time? I know you won't rest until you fill this house up with every denomination known to man."

"If you will knock off the theatrics, John."

"I'm not the one stretching this conversation out. Can you please get to the point?"

"We have a priest who needs a place to live."

I was stunned. My voice reflected it. "A priest? A Catholic priest?"

"You know of any other kind?" the Bishop said with great tiredness in his voice.

“You are giving me an assistant? Or someone older? A retired priest, perhaps?”

“You may have met him at some point during the last few years. Father Barry St. Stephen.”

“Father Barry? Yes, he’s a young man. I met him at a seminar last year. I think he’s only been a priest for a short time.”

“Yes, about three years. He has been an assistant over at the Church of the Forsaken in Sliver City ever since he was ordained.

I eyed the Bishop suspiciously. “You know I have never liked the name of that church. Were there too many St. Marys in the diocese?”

The Bishop ignored my digression. I got back on task.

"Why would Fr. Barry be moving in here? What could possibly be going on?"

"There is much, I'm afraid."

"These long pauses between speaking do not help, Kevin." As was our custom, he was delaying and I was prompting.

"It's not what you think." He was doing a poor job of comforting me.

"What I think? You can read my mind?" I knew the Bishop had many talents, but being a psychic was not one of them.

"I can't read your mind, John," the Bishop answered.

"That's a good thing right now, Kevin." We both would agree on that.

"I did think, having met Fr. Barry, you would assume this is about . . . you know."

My outrage was too strong to hide. "Let's get past that real quick. Yes, I know what Fr. Barry's sexual orientation is. Being gay does not mean he can't be an effective priest. And it certainly does not mean he's going to sexually assault people. I understand that. Do you?"

"Well, some people assume that one leads to another." The Bishop was correct about what people thought.

"Some people, bless them, are blooming idiots." I emphasized the word "idiots" – another example of my need to improve my behavior.

"Father Barry and I have been meeting quite a bit lately. He is confused about what he wants to do." With this statement I could see both sadness and frustration in the Bishop's face. I hated to see such a great man feel sad.

"Do? Do about what? Let's put all our cards on the table, Kevin." I tried to encourage him to continue his thoughts.

"He is unsure about whether or not he wants to continue in the priesthood." With this declaration Bishop O'Reilly looked like a beaten man. The scandals of the last few years had taken a vicious toll. While we did not see eye to eye on any number of subjects, the Bishop was a good man. He had dedicated his life to God while I was a toddler still learning how to tie my shoes. What really bothered me was not those seeking justice. Without question there were those who were abused, and they deserved their day in court. The real problem was the anti-Catholic media who never tired of publicly continuing the anguish of the victims. No organization withstood the merciless pummeling that the Catholic Church did. To me, the media was not concerned reporting the news. They were consumed with vilifying the church founded by Christ.

"This bothers me, Kevin. I do not understand why Father Barry would be treated this way. He struck me as a very good man. I saw a gentleness in him that I wish all men had. Heaven knows I could use a dose." I knew there would not be any disagreement my last declaration.

"We haven't yet got to the bottom of it. I think it is largely because of how some, a very few, actually, parishioners have treated him. Some of the people in his parish exclude him from activities that normally all priests would be invited to." The Bishop's reluctance to discuss the subject was understandable. He was starting to open up a bit more now.

"It sounds like junior high school. I am not saying Father Barry should not be affected by such behavior, but if you wear the collar you have to be ready for that kind of thing. There must be more going on."

"There is. Some parents have complained when Father Barry visits their kid's catechism class. There are those who get up and leave a meeting when Father Barry walks in." Now the Bishop was staring at the floor as he spoke. I longed to take some of his burden from him.

"Wow. They hate him because he's gay?" It was unbelievable what I was hearing.

"I try to give them some benefit of the doubt. I think they are afraid of him, afraid of what he might do." The Bishop stared into space as he spoke.

"That is truly insane. Father Barry is a holy man."

"Listen, John. Look at the media and how they have portrayed priests the last ten years. We have a few rogue priests, 'criminals masquerading as priests,' to quote you, and the media makes it look like we're all like that. Any time a priest sneezes and doesn't cover his cough it's on the front page. And what is worse, the stories make it look like all priests are as guilty as the few who commit these vile acts."

We had covered this territory a number of times and it was always unpleasant. I felt we had to acknowledge past mistakes and not sweep them under the rug. Still, it was a bitter medicine to be continually reminded.

"We have discussed many times how the Church did a poor job of handling the situation initially. I know you are sick of hearing it, but keeping it fresh in our minds might help prevent a reoccurrence."

"Such evil within the Catholic Church threw us all for a loop and yes, we could have done a better job. But that's no reason to persecute those who have and would never do any harm." The Bishop was absolutely correct.

"Well, part of having this job means you have to be able to take an occasional beating. I will say it once more. Father Barry should be able to take the heat."

"It's not just that. The people who have behaved so poorly have started spreading rumors. Father Barry can't walk down the street anymore without people calling him names – sometimes under their breath and sometimes out loud. It seems more and more people believe whatever crazy rumors they hear. You know how gossip spreads, regardless of there being no truth behind it."

"Have you thought that it will further fuel the rumors if Father Barry suddenly disappears from his church?" I just did not want to feed the fires of gossip.

"I have told Father Barry that if he does take a sabbatical, he will need to make a statement to his parishioners – I want complete transparency. If people are going to gossip they will have to do so knowing full well they are spreading lies. Right now he is due a month of vacation. That would give him some time to decide whether to go on Sabbatical. I would expect he would want to help out while he is here. If it is okay with you for him to be here." His last sentence was a request I did not need to consider for long.

I appreciated the Bishop giving me control of whether or not Father Barry would be here. It was a measure of respect I was unprepared for.

"Mom keeps all the rooms ready to be lived in. Today or tomorrow soon enough?"

I felt very good about the look of relief on the Bishop's face.

"What would be his duties here?"

"Whatever you and he agree on. This is your parish. Use him as you see fit. Remember, though, he is to have time to reflect on his vocation. You do have a way with bringing out the best in people. I am not going to micromanage the situation."

"Thank you for that. We'll work something out as we go. Things work out best if we put them in God's hands and provide support."

I walked the Bishop out to his car. He made major strides in our relationship today. I don't know why, but it seemed he was more giving and on my side. On the other hand, maybe I was just maturing – thirty years later than most people.

As the Bishop and I spoke at his car, Carl drove up. Sensing the conversation was significant, Carl only said hello to the Bishop and then excused himself. I was always impressed by his ability to size up a situation and act accordingly. Today was no exception.

Our conversation went on a few more minutes. It was unique in that we wound up discussing general matters instead of business. It was the first time I recalled that we had ever a conversation as two normal people. Without the stress of work-related drama, we got on pretty well.

My next appointment pulled up in his car. The Bishop was considerate enough to say a quick goodbye and drove off. The parishioner was having a tough time. He was going through the experience of what we call a “dark” time. He was struggling with the very idea that God existed – an all too common problem that many people grappled with and the very essence of why priests were kept busy in every parish.

After an hour of serious listening on my part while he processed his thoughts, my parishioner went on his way. I think we made some progress but scheduled another appointment for the next week. There was time now to relax a bit before dinner. I sat down on the couch next to Mom. Carl sat in what had become his easy chair and started talking.

“Well, there’s the air of the mysterious floating around here, John. Care to share what’s going on?”

I rushed to the point. “We are having a houseguest.”

“I thought I was your houseguest.” Carl smiled.

Mom could not let that go. “Carl, you’re family.”

“Here I was hoping John was going to say that. I have been praying for that,” Carl lightly jousted.

“It must be those Lutheran prayers. They don’t work so well,” I shrugged.

Mom crossed her arms. That meant it was time to move on.

So," Carl continued, "is the Bishop moving another priest here? I'll be outnumbered."

"Yes, Father Barry St. Stephen is his name. He's a younger priest. A very nice man person. I think we will get along fine."

"So, he's your assistant?" A reasonable conclusion from Carl, but a wrong one.

"You don't need an assistant," Mom interjected.

"Father Barry is going to be here on a vacation of sorts. Really a kind of mini-sabbatical. He has some reservations about his vocation because some of his parishioners are treating him poorly and spreading rumors about his behavior."

"What kind of behavior?" Carl was worried.

"It is not behavior, it is just rumors. Father Barry is gay. He has not, to my knowledge, been sexually active. However, some seem to think being gay leads to pedophilia."

Carl sighed. "You must be kidding."

"That is sad," Mom added.

"No, I'm not kidding and, yes, it is sad. In this day and age there are many who waste no opportunity to criticize the priesthood. Truth is, the Church did not handle the sexual abuse crisis well when it arose and is now paying a steep penalty."

We sat silently contemplating the situation that was emerging around us. As we did so, John Paul walked into the room.

"Hey, man – it looks like there was somebody important here today. And now we are having a meeting. A big sorry I'm late," John Paul said as he plopped down next to me on the couch.

"You're not late. You can't be late for a meeting you weren't invited to." Sometimes John Paul needed straight talk.

"Since you're a member of the family you are invited." Mom ended my attempt at straight talk.

"Whoa, man. I'm getting mixed messages here." John Paul seemed confused.

It was easier to give in. He would need to know anyway. "We're having a new priest come to live here, John Paul. His name is Father Barry."

"What's his story, guys?" John Paul had no reservations about prying.

"Story? What do you mean?" I was stalling for time.

"Why are they sending them here? We already got a full house. I don't know if I want to get used to someone new. "John Paul scratched his chin as he spoke. Somehow he knew something was going on.

"It's a long story." The longer I stalled, the more difficult this was going to be.

John Paul quit scratching his chin and snapped his fingers. He had a Eureka moment.

"He's in some kind of trouble! Isn't he?" he exclaimed.

"That's enough for now." I tried to put an end to the conversation.

“He is being treated poorly because he’s gay,” Mom began explaining.

“Well, I’m straight,” John Paul announced. “He isn’t going to hit on me, is he?”

“I don’t think you need to worry,” I assured John Paul. “He is still firmly committed to his vow of celibacy.”

“He sells what?” John Paul asked.

“Celibacy.”

Annoyed, John Paul repeated himself. “I asked you, what does he sell?”

For some reason I looked at Mom for assistance. She had a way of reaching John Paul. But she was having none of this.

“I have a bedroom to prepare, gentlemen. Excuse me.” She quickly left the room

John Paul looked to me for more information. “Never mind,” was the best I could do.

CHAPTER THIRTEEN

Two days later, Father Barry arrived with two large suitcases in hand. The fact that he traveled so lightly told me material possessions were not important to him, always impressive for a man in his career.

I welcomed Barry in to the house. Mom prepared coffee and some sweet rolls while I showed him to his room. He was as polite a person as I had ever known. His short-cropped hair complimented his tall, slender build. He was quite reserved in his mannerisms and quiet spoken. I could not imagine how anyone would not enjoy his presence.

We sat down in the kitchen and munched on mom's delicious snacks. Barry was attentive and respectful. He made a wonderful first impression.

"So that's about all there is to know about this parish." I concluded. "If you feel comfortable saying Mass I'll be glad to schedule you in to either daily or the weekend. And I think some of the parish would appreciate having another priest for confession on Saturday afternoon.

Barry seemed appreciative of my offer. "Thank you, John. Right now, until I get my head straightened out, I don't think it is right for me to say Mass."

"As you wish." I hoped he would change his mind but was not about to push him to do something he was not ready to do. We sat back in our kitchen chairs and relaxed. A nice calm filled the room.

Proving that things can change quickly, John Paul rushed into the kitchen carrying some tools. He grabbed a glass out of the cupboard, filled it with water and sucked it down as if he had just completed a forty-year trek through the desert. John Paul put the glass in the sink and, much to my relief, began to walk back outside. Then he stopped and stared at Father Barry.

"Uh, Father Barry, this is John Paul. He does some handyman work around here. He bunks in the garage." My mind busily whirred around trying to think of a way to tell Barry that John Paul tended to say things without thinking. I took too long.

Barry put his hand up to shake hands. For a second it appeared we were going to have a normal action take place. A sense of relief fell over me.

"You must be the gay guy!" John Paul exclaimed.

I put my face in my hands. I had hoped for a better impression but deep down expected this. Barry smiled.

"I see my fame has preceded me. It is good to meet you, John Paul. That, by the way, is a nice name."

Ignoring Barry's statement, John Paul continued, "We had a meeting about you."

"And what did you decide?" Barry continued to smile though he looked a bit worried. His calm, laid-back demeanor was a joy to observe. He held this position in the palm of his hand.

"The man here told me not to worry."

I felt my day collapsing around me.

"Worry about what? Wait, I think I'd rather not know." Barry laughed.

"John Paul," I said, trying to refocus his thoughts, "did my mother give you a project to do today?"

"No, she just said to stay out of the house because the two of you had to talk."

The entertainment value of this conversation and the situation I was in was not lost on Barry. I could have charged him admission.

"Mom asked you to stay out of the house. And you realize you are in the house?" I was trying to educate by taking one step at a time.

"I wanted to see what was going on."

"Well, Barry, at least you are getting a good idea of what goes on around here every day."

Barry leaned back and folded his hands. His smile got wider.

"I am starting to think I will like it here very much."

John Paul had exceeded his limit for being quiet, which was about thirty seconds long. “Sorry, dudes. These kinds of meetings bore me. I’m going outside.”

“Interesting man,” Barry understated. “So he handles the maintenance around the house?”

“That, and he constantly makes me question my sanity.”

“You have Carl and me to help you with that,” Mom chimed in.

“I am anxious to meet Reverend Carl. It is so impressive that two men of different faiths are living together. So you have become good friends? At least that is what Bishop O’Reilly told me.”

“The Bishop, as always speaks the truth. Actually, it was his idea. Carl is a wonderful human being, a great friend, and has made my daily life better. Don’t ever repeat that to Carl or I will excommunicate you.”

“There’s a lot of people in line in front of you wanting to do that,” Barry laughed.

“If there is one thing I know, it is that we need good men like you as priests.”

“If we could be frank, John, I want to make sure the two of you are cool with me living here. I know the Bishop didn’t give you any choice, but if you don’t want me, it’s okay to be honest. There is nothing more disruptive to a family than a stranger showing up and moving in. I won’t say anything to the Bishop. I’ll just quietly find a different place.”

I was so engrossed in the conversation I had not heard Carl drive up. He walked in the house just as I finished my thought out loud.

“When change happens to me I have found that fighting it makes me miserable. Accepting change and embracing it as an adventure makes life exciting and richer. If there's one thing I've discovered in my life, it's that the more diversity I embrace the more fascinating my life becomes."

"I think he's talking about me," Carl said. "Hi, I am Carl Carter. I am very glad to meet you."

Carl walked over and shook Barry's hand.

"Not just you, Carl, am I talking about." I smiled at Carl and he gave me a knowing look. He was a perfect foil for me.

"The real question, especially important to me, Barry is – are you comfortable living here with two middle-aged curmudgeons?" Carl put this question in a humorous way but it was a vital query to put on the table.

Barry had a way of looking you right in the eye when he spoke. It gave me a lot of confidence that I could trust him. "I used spend a lot of time praying that things would turn out exactly the way I wanted. Then I discovered that true happiness comes when you accept what God has given you. Once you accept His will, the rest falls into place."

"Hmmm," Carl spoke softly, almost to himself, "that line of thought has brought me great comfort since my Betty died."

"I think, Barry that we are lucky to have you living here. I am looking forward to spending time with you. And who knows, maybe we'll get some work out of you." I winked.

"I would like to at least meet some of your flock," Barry said. "People will probably be curious about me. It will give them a chance to know me."

"I have just the ticket," I said, as I realized what was on my calendar tonight. "Have you ever been to a Knights meeting?"

“Knights? You mean Knights of Columbus?” Barry wondered.

“Yes, I am filling in for the regular chaplain tonight. Since this area is rural, we incorporate a lot of small towns in our district. You would have an opportunity to meet a many different people. Good people.”

“I was inducted into the Knights shortly after I was ordained,” Barry said. “With everything going on while I was getting my feet wet, so to speak, I never had time to get involved. Would it be okay for me attend the meeting?”

“I want you there tonight. We have a great man in charge who runs a tight meeting, so we take care of business quickly.”

“What Johnny means is there will be plenty of time for drinking a beer or two afterward,” Mom explained.

“The woman knows me all too well,” I admitted.

Carl was interested in the conversation but seemed worried about speaking up. I wanted to know what he was thinking so gave a welcoming look. It worked.

"The Knights," he wondered out loud. "I am curious about that organization. They are not exactly politically correct these days, are they? I mean Columbus is not the universally admired person he once was." Carl was being honest and open with his feelings, not negative. He was asking valid points.

"We celebrate Columbus' role in bringing the faith to the new world," I explained. "The culture of the time encouraged adventure, exploration and spreading the word of God. We acknowledge that, as is the case with every man, he was not perfect. And important to remember, we do not meet just to honor a man. The organization makes a significant, positive contribution to our society. Other than the Shriners, I cannot think of an organization that does so much charitable work."

“We Lutherans do our share, too, I think,” Carl added, valiantly standing up for his own.

“I would not doubt that. The Knights I know donate a lot of time and effort to make the world a better place. They are prayerful people who celebrate the family. We are better off with the Knights as a healthy, productive force for good. That much I know for sure.”

The evening went very well indeed. It would be inappropriate for me to record details about the meeting, but I experienced great satisfaction with how my brother Knights treated Barry. Not for long was he a stranger to them. And Barry, though naturally an introvert, handled himself very well during the after-meeting. How could one not enjoy oneself when enjoying a brew with good-natured fellows?

The next several days went better than I could ever have imagined. Barry still did not feel comfortable saying Mass or performing duties associated with the priesthood. He did a lot of work around the house including maintenance requests that I had previously asked, without success, John Paul to do.

We woke at different times so never saw each other in the morning, but it was fun to have the four of us sitting around the dinner table every evening. The conversations were so lively it was reminded me of my college days. One of the best parts was Mom could take a break from cooking. Barry proved to be a gourmet cook who enjoyed treating us to all sorts of exotic foods. And his expertise was not limited to only entrées; his desserts were, well, sinful. My expanding waistline proved there was a price associated with sin.

It was the day after Barry treated us with the most decadent cheesecake of my life that I was sitting in the office reading one of Bishop O'Reilly's communiqués that he sent out monthly to all the priests. I looked up to see Mom standing in the doorway. She did not look pleased.

"Johnny, I just had a phone call requesting an emergency meeting with you. I checked your calendar and you do have time this afternoon."

"Sure, no problem. I was going to do some catching up but seeing a parishioner is more important. Who is it?"

"Mrs. Satane," Mom grimly replied. Her facial expression said it all.

"I have not seen her in church the last few weeks. She always sits in the same place. I wasn't sure she was still a member here." I did not mention to Mom about Carl's encounter with her. "Did she say what the emergency was?"

"She did not say and you know I never ask. A lot of what people come to talk about is personal. I am here to help, not chase people away."

"I appreciate all you do. Go ahead and schedule her for two o'clock."

Taking a deep breath, I considered what Mrs. Satane wanted. Whenever we spoke she had a definite agenda. The fact that she had considered leaving the Catholic Church, apparently because of her unhappiness with me, made me question if I was adequately performing my job. Trying to think reasonably I confronted the fact that she was difficult for many people to work with. I did not share with Carl that many parishioners had complained about Mrs. Satane.

I took advantage of the time before our meeting to pray. Time and again I have found that my limited intelligence is no match for the hurdles in my life. I turn things over to God and He does the heavy lifting.

My peaceful day came to a close at two o'clock. Mom showed Mrs. Satane into my office.

"Mrs. Satane, Luci. Good afternoon," I greeted her.

Mrs. Satane's stone face gave no indication that she heard me. She quickly sat down.

"How may I help you today?" I wondered.

"Father, first of all I guess I should thank you for seeing me on such short notice."

"Of course." She was being polite. That was a good start.

"My mother said that you had an emergency. It worked out very fortunately as this is the day of the week I visit the hospital. We do not have any parishioners in there this week so I have some free time."

Her face soured. "Oh, I thought you were supposed to care about everyone, not just Catholics."

"You are correct, Mrs. Satane. Thank you for pointing that out." I remained calm. There was no point in telling her that I always went to the hospital regardless of whether there was anyone I knew. Not having any parishioners meant I did not have any appointments and could arrive at the hospital later in the day.

We experienced an uncomfortable pause. I could see in her eyes a fiery glow. She was checking her ammunition.

"This is very difficult for me to say, Father," she began.

Patience was never a strength for me. Especially when something was going to be unpleasant, I preferred to get it over with.

"Your family, Mrs. Satane. Is everyone doing well?" I had to get things moving.

"My family? What makes you ask that?"

"I am wondering what your emergency is, Mrs. Satane. Oftentimes someone will come to see me because of a family issue." I knew explaining would not help.

"My family is doing extremely well. We are one of the premier families in the city of Blessing, you know. Of course, my husband is such a well-respected business owner."

My eyes started to glass over at the nonsense shooting out of her mouth. I knew it would get worse before it got better.

"And my *daughter.*" She emphasized so loudly everyone within a mile would hear. "Everyone says my daughter is the most beautiful young woman in the city. All the girls wish they could be her. But that is what happens when you come from a family of high status."

I do not think I had ever felt such a desire to vomit. It was a good thing I did not each much for lunch or I might not have been able to control myself.

"Mrs. Satane? Is there something you want to talk about today? The emergency?" I was ready to run out of the room screaming. As it turns out, I should have.

"My sister, Jezzie. We are very close. We talk several times a week. Jezzie is my younger sister but we are so much alike, people think we are twins."

I nodded. If there was a point to any of this it was beyond my comprehension.

"Are you following me, Father?" she asked. I was not.

"So . . . something is wrong with your sister that you want to discuss?"

"Nothing is wrong with my sister. She is a pillar of the community, just like I am."

I wondered if she would mind if I took out a book and started to read it while waiting for her to come to the reason for her visit. It appeared I would have time to get through a good-sized novel. Finally, she spoke and things became very clear.

"My sister lives in Sliver City," she exclaimed. "Of course, being a good Catholic, she is active in the church. Much more active than most."

“The church in Sliver City is the Church of the Forsaken, is it not?” The train had left the depot. I just wanted it to fly off the tracks and get it over with.

“Yes. You know they have two priests there. Father Joseph and his assistant. I believe his name is Father Barry.”

“Mmmm hmmm,” I agreed.

“My sister, who would never spread an unsubstantiated rumor, has told me that Father Barry is going to move to this parish. She has also told me a great deal about this Father Barry. A great deal.”

“Mmmm hmmm,” I repeated.

The fire in her eyes was growing. The look on her face was unyielding.

“Actually, Mrs. Satane, Father Barry has already moved into our parish house. We are fortunate to have such a good, decent priest in residence here.”

“My sister tells me he is . . . well . . . not normal.”

“I have been alive fifty years. Twenty-five of that has been spent as a priest. I am not sure I have ever met anyone who meets the standard of normal.”

“That’s not what I meant.” She spat out the words.

“I know it’s not what you meant,” I assured her.

“You are aware he’s not . . . ” She could not quite come up with the term she was looking for.

“Interested in women?” I attempted to help her.

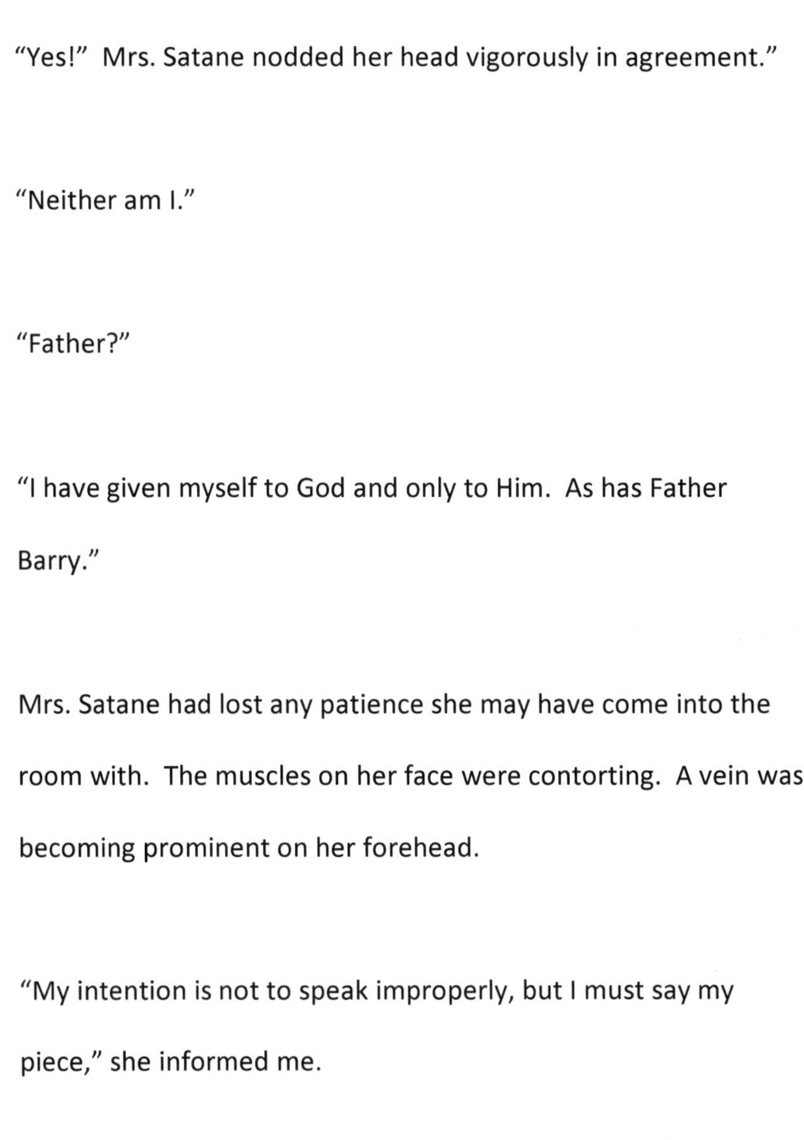

"Yes!" Mrs. Satane nodded her head vigorously in agreement."

"Neither am I."

"Father?"

"I have given myself to God and only to Him. As has Father Barry."

Mrs. Satane had lost any patience she may have come into the room with. The muscles on her face were contorting. A vein was becoming prominent on her forehead.

"My intention is not to speak improperly, but I must say my piece," she informed me.

"*Peace* seems to be the last thing on your mind, but go ahead." I was only being honest.

She finally spewed forth her pent-up emotions. "I will not, nor will I allow any of my fellow parishioners, to have anything to do with Father Barry."

"You will not allow?" Her nerve was world-class. "We need to discuss that momentarily. First, though, please tell me how your fellow parishioners know about Father Barry? Do they have sisters who live in Sliver City also? Surely you haven't been spreading gossip?"

"I feel it is my DUTY to inform people as to what goes on in my church!"

"Silly me. I thought it was God's church."

"It is, and someone has to take a stand for decency since you won't."

"I am standing for decency right now."

"I will not allow you to permit that man in this parish."

I folded my hands as if I was praying. Prayer was the furthest thing from my mind. I suspected a headline in the newspaper about a priest bodily throwing a parishioner out the front door would be met with displeasure from Bishop O'Reilly. Then again, it would not be the first time I did something to displease him.

"Please understand that I am the priest in this parish. I make decisions about what is and is not appropriate."

"You are not capable of making an appropriate decision." The insults just did not stop with this woman.

"Regardless what you may think, the choice is mine." I refused to back down.

"So the Bible means nothing to you?"

"The Bible is one of the basic tenets of the Catholic religion. Show me where it states I should humiliate someone because of their orientation."

"It is quite clear that homosexuality is evil."

"The Bible refers to acting on the impulse to have sex. Or can you show me where it says otherwise?" I picked the Bible off my desk and tried to hand it to her. "What is your favorite verse? Where would I find it? Corinthians? One of the Gospels?"

Mrs. Satane pushed the Bible away with the back of her hand. "Stupid book. I don't have the time to read it."

"You have never read the Bible?" I queried.

"I am a busy woman," she replied. "All I need to know is evil must be destroyed. We have great power if we just decide to use it. Overwhelming force is the only way to destroy."

"You know Jesus used to teach with parables. A story my professor taught in the seminary comes to mind. It seems a man lived a good long life and died. At heaven's gate he told St. Peter he missed his house and farm so much he could not go in to heaven. Jesus came out to speak with him and you know what he said?"

"He screamed at the man and ordered to get in now or else!" she shouted.

"No, that is not how the story ends. Jesus gently took the man's hand and asked him to take a look inside the gate. The man did so and saw his house and farm there waiting for him."

"What is the point of that stupid story?" she wondered.

"Gentleness is the best way to persuade people, not brute force. There is a Bible verse that describes God as a gentle whisper."

Mrs. Satane rolled her eyes. She was intent on making certain I knew how much despised me.

"What does any of that have to do with Father Barry spreading his wickedness in this parish?"

"Father Barry has not been spreading wickedness. Far from it. His short time here so far has been a blessing to me."

Mrs. Satane curled her lip. "I see. So you have succumbed. I believe the only thing left to do is to contact Bishop O'Reilly. He needs to know what kind of outfit you have going on here."

"You are more than welcome to contact the Bishop." Obviously, she did not know he was behind Father Barry's move here.

"And I will make sure he knows about all the other things going on here. Do not think for a minute we don't know what is going on here. First you have this protestant living here. And that man, that weirdo, who lives in your garage. These people are Catholics. If you believed the Catholic religion was the true faith you would throw them out on the street where they belong."

"Because I follow the Catholic religion I cannot throw them out on the street," I corrected her.

"There is no reason for me to stay here. Rest assured I will contact the Bishop and if he does not take care of you, the Pope will be next."

"As you wish." I did not mind the threats so much because it sounded like she was going to leave.

She stood so violently her chair flew back. "And once we get a good priest in here I will make sure he fires that youth minister!"

"The youth minister told me she made it very clear to your daughter that she was welcome to return any time. If she is too embarrassed to face the youth minister, she should know she does not have to say anything if she shows up at the next youth meeting. No apologies necessary."

"APOLOGIES!? My daughter has nothing to apologize for. I have never been so insulted." She turned, threw open the door, and stormed out. I felt lucky to be alive.

With every step Mrs. Satane took down the hallway, her pace quickened. The force of air caused her hair to fly up into a point. She pivoted on her right foot and headed into the kitchen. I heard a loud thunk. Worried about what had just occurred, I ran into the room and saw Barry sitting on the kitchen floor. Apparently, my fleeing parishioner had collided with Barry and sent him sprawling. He seemed okay, though a little dazed by the surprise collision. He looked up at her and offered a little smile. I think he wanted to assure that he was okay and not to feel guilty about splattering him.

"Ma'am, you have the best of me, I'm afraid. I hope you are not injured." Typical Barry, more concerned about the assaulter than himself.

Mrs. Satane glared at him. She understood immediately who he was. Apologies were not her style, especially to someone she despised. It did not matter that she did not know him, she still hated him.
Barry, of course, had no idea as to what transpired at our meeting. He made another attempt to greet her.

"I was hoping to meet some of the people of this parish, but not in this way." He smiled.

There was still no reaction. She straightened her blouse and pretended to dust herself off. The polite thing to do was to introduce them.

“Father Barry St. Stephens, this is one of my parishioners, Mrs. Luci Satane,” I offered.

Barry got up and brushed his hands together.

“May I call you Luci?” he asked.

“No, you may not,” she commanded. “My name, if you must repeat it, is MRS. Satane.”

Barry studied her mannerisms carefully. He was a master of sizing up people, far more advanced in the trade than I was at his age.

“Mrs. Satane, it is a pleasure to meet you.”

"Humppff," was her response.

"I look forward to meeting as many of the people in this parish as I can. Tell me. I love to cook. What do you think of organizing a get-together where everyone brings their favorite dish?" He looked at her eagerly for a response.

"I am not surprised you enjoy cooking," she coldly responded.

"Really?"

"Really. Now I really must be going."

There was no need to prolong this anymore. Time spent with her would continue to be unpleasant and there was no reason to subject Barry to her special form of pain. I escorted her to the door. Returning to Barry, I felt something should be said but did not know what. He took the lead, using his dry wit.

“Charming woman,” Barry brightly said, a mischievous smile on his face.

“Yes, it is so good the two of you had some quality time to spend together.”

“That is what you consider to be quality time?” Barry asked, his face filled with shock.

“Put it this way, you got off lucky,” I assured him.

There arose a racket from outside that instantly caught our attention. Without a word we both ran outside. Mrs. Satane, her supply of anger still at least half-full, was screaming at John Paul. The poor man had been walking by her car with some gardening tools in his hand when she accosted him.

“You bum!” she screamed. “You welfare trash. Do not look at me like that.”

"Lady-person, I do not know you are talking about. I was just walking to the garden to do some weeding."

She turned to me and continued her rant.

"Get this thing away from me. He was looking at me with sex on his mind. I know that look."

"Mrs. Satane, that is an accusation without merit. You cannot accuse people of things. It is not right," I corrected her.

"Lady-person," John Paul repeated, then paused – not a common event for him – before he finished his sentence, "what crawled up your butt?"

How I would have treasured a video recording of that scene. Her response was to loudly use words that I, portraying myself as a humble priest, am not comfortable writing here.

The woman, or lady-person, as John Paul so eloquently named her, drove away at a speed far above what would be safe.

"Are you okay, John Paul?" I asked. It was not clear to me whether he had hurt feelings from his encounter.

"Yeah, man. I think that woman needs to spend more time with you holy dudes."

Barry and I looked at each. We were silent, but we both were thinking the last thing either of us wanted was to spend more time with her.

Barry stayed outside to help John Paul with his work. I went inside and finished up my paperwork. Later on, while waiting for Mom to finish up dinner preparations, Barry, Carl, and I sat in the living room.

Carl asked about my day and I told him we had a difficult meeting with a parishioner. It would have been inappropriate to go into details about what she had said about Barry.

"I ran into the woman John is talking about. Literally," Barry stated.

"More accurately, she ran into you," I countered.

"There seems to be a lot of anger emanating from that poor woman. I wish I knew what the problem was so I could help." Barry compassionately sighed.

"There are many stories I could tell you about some of the people in this parish. But the Seal of the Confessional prevents it," I said jokingly.

"Let's hear a cheer for the Seal!" Barry gleefully shouted.

Carl stroked the whiskers on his beard thoughtfully. He wanted to say something and thankfully he felt comfortable to do so. “Do you know non-Catholics have an overwhelming curiosity about what goes on in the confessional?”

“We can solve that mystery in a minute. Kneel down and tell me your sins.” I encouraged him with a broad smile on my face.

“You know I can’t do that,” Carl responded slyly.

“Because you’re Lutheran?” Barry innocently asked.

“Because I don’t have any sins,” Carl explained.

“Lying is a sin where I come from. Of course I come from the church Jesus started. That hardly compares with your background,” I replied.

Barry laughed and said, "I feel like a spectator at a wrestling match."

"We're just getting warmed up," Carl bragged.

"I hope no blood splatters this way," Barry said.

"No worries, I always use kid gloves. MY religion requires me to be meek," Carl stated triumphantly.

"Your Bible says that, too?" I asked with shock. "I guess there are a few parts Martin Luther didn't re-write."

"Re-write, no, he was too busy following what is written in the Bible. I only wish Catholics followed the Bible as closely as Martin Luther. It is foolproof." Carl was more than treading water. I was proud of him.

"Funny you should mention the term 'foolproof,'" I added.

Barry jumped in feet first. “I remember in the Seminary we learned a saying. You can make something foolproof. But you cannot make it damn-fool proof.”

This gave us pause to reflect. Carl and I surveyed each other for a clue as to what the other was thinking. Carl was first to break the quiet.

“What is that supposed to mean?” Carl asked.

“Or are you calling us fools?” I said, with as much false indignity as I could.

Barry stuck his finger in the air. An important point was about to be made. “Another thing they used to tell us. If the shoe fits, wear it.”

Carl and I exchanged knowing smiles.

“I think we have a third for our choral group,” Carl confirmed.

“None too soon,” I reflected. “I was getting tired of doing all the heavy lifting.”

The next ten minutes brought a continuing lively discussion about all things religious, ending with a tacit agreement between myself and Barry that Minnesota had far better relief pitching than any New York team.

CHAPTER FOURTEEN

Three weeks flew by. Perhaps it was luck. More likely it was the will of the Almighty. The four of us established a loving, close-knit family in no time at all. Always content and happy with my station in life, I found myself more so than I could have ever imagined. Several days each week I stopped what I was doing and thanked God for all the change that had occurred. Most of all, I thanked Him for not letting me make a mess of things by fighting the unstoppable revolution that had transformed into my life.

The undeniable fact is Mom's life was better than it had been since dad died. That was what was really important to me. I thought of how during the last few years she had made her life all about me. She deserved more in her life than having to be the caretaker for a grown man with an adolescent mentality.

Change to me had always meant loss of control. I feared change. I embraced comfort. A life lesson of abundant value had been taught. I was a humbled but grateful student.

A free hour in my morning schedule gave me time to contemplate Father Barry's position. He had fit in the parish beautifully. He had an appetite for work that I had never known. Most of his time was spent on various church committees or providing chaplaincy services at the Knights of Columbus Hall. Any free time after that was spent assisting John Paul with maintenance work on the church and house.

For the first time since I came to St. Jude, I thought about how helpful it would be to have an assistant. Father Barry would be a perfect addition to this church. Our church always seemed too small for a second priest, but his level of energy re-wrote all the rules.

I went through the mail while composing a letter in my head to the Bishop. As much as I enjoyed my housemates, it was relaxing when I had the place to myself. With Carl at his office at the Lutheran Church and John Paul heaven only knew where, a rare gift of silence had been bestowed. Just as Carl's name passed through my thoughts I saw that he had a letter from the Lutheran Seminary. I mused that a person of his character would be perfect for the education of his students.

Continuing composing a letter to the Bishop proved challenging but enjoyable. He would need strong justification for assigning Barry here. It would take every bit of writing ability I had. This meant of course that I might have make myself beholden to the good Bishop. It would be worth it. Barry brought such a breath of fresh air wherever he went, that no cost would be too much.

My fantasy was interrupted by the unpleasant ring of my phone. Mom was out visiting one of her friends, so I answered the phone.

"Hello, Father Krentz speaking," I pleasantly declared.

"JOHN," Carl shouted, "thank goodness you are all right." A breath of relief followed his exclamation.

"Why wouldn't I be all right?" I puzzled.

"I just had someone stop by my church. They told me someone died at the Knights of Columbus Hall an hour ago." Carl's voice got a bit calmer, but some fear still gripped him. "He told me that it looked like a priest was being carried into the ambulance. I was shaking so hard I could hardly dial the phone."

"Barry!" my voice trembled. "Barry went down to the hall this morning to help with a painting project. I have to run down there, Carl!" I cried out as I set the phone down.

Only with great difficulty was I able to keep from exceeding the speed limit on my way to the hospital. I knew that my personal concerns did not outweigh the necessity to be a safe driver. I pulled into the hospital parking lot. With great gratitude for the special parking place set aside for clergy, I stopped my car and hurried into the hospital.

"Please, can you tell me anything about the man who was just admitted?" I begged the receptionist.

"Father, we cannot give out any information, but since you are clergy you can walk back to the Emergency Room."

I stepped quickly. Horrible thoughts crossed my mind. I cursed myself for not taking time during the drive here to pray. Every personal foible I had ever committed came back to me as I started blaming myself for what happened to Barry. After all, it was I who insisted he come down to the Knights of Columbus Hall in the first place. How I would ever forgive myself was beyond me.

I made the turn into the ER and immediately bumped into . . .

Barry?

"BARRY?!" I exclaimed as the force of my body bumped him back into the wall.

Barry was dumbfounded to see me. That, plus the fact that I had knocked the wind out of him, seemed to confuse him all the more.

"John?" he asked, "what are you doing here?"

"Carl called me. He said that someone had died at the hall and that a priest was seen being put into an ambulance. I feared the worse. So if it wasn't you, who was it?"

Barry forced a little smile.

“Thank you for your concern. Perhaps we should sit down over there. I don’t think I can stand another beating from anyone barreling down the hallway.”

“I am sorry.”

“Not a problem,” Barry assured me as we sat down. “Let me start at the beginning.”

His calm demeanor made me feel at ease. The man was born to be priest.

“I was the person who was helped into the ambulance. I bumped my head while giving CPR to one of the volunteers. My technique is sloppy to say the least, and I was so vigorous with my strokes that my head hit the wall. It was actually kind of embarrassing. I was carrying out some paint when a man walking up to the hall collapsed against the outside wall. I hollered for assistance and then began CPR. I was doing fine for the first few minutes but got pretty tired and that is when I hit my head. Fortunately, the ambulance arrived just as it happened. The paramedics said since I was a bit dazed I should ride in the ambulance to the hospital. Someone must have seen them help me in."

For the first time in several minutes my heart stopped pounding in my chest. I felt great relief.

"The person who died?"

"God was good to his family today," Barry asserted. "He is alive now."

"Thanks be to God and also to you for your good work," I complimented.

"The paramedics did say that I kept enough blood flowing in him that they were able to shock him back into life." Barry paused. I could tell he was not sure if he should say out loud what he was thinking. “Do you ever wonder about how things work out?”

I smiled and nodded. “Go on.”

“Had I not come here that poor man would have lain there for a long time. He would have died. My pain with what I went through in Sliver City brought life to this man.”

“I don’t believe in coincidences, either,” I assured him.

We sat silently for a minute. I realized something.

“He was going to the Knights Hall – he must be a Catholic. He must be one of my parishioners. Do you know what his name is?”

“I do now. I just spoke with him before you blasted into me,” Barry kidded me. “His name is Peter Satane.”

"Mr. Satane?"

"Yes. Was that woman who knocked me down a few weeks ago . . ."

"Yes, that is his wife."

"Do you think that will change her opinion of me?" Barry wondered.

"No," I painfully but honestly answered.

"Well, can we speak confidentially? One priest consulting another?" Barry asked.

"Of course," I declared.

"Mr. Satane told me he had a near death experience."

“I have always been fascinated by those,” I said. “Sometimes they cause major life changes.”

“Well, he had an epiphany all right,” Barry told me. Mr. Satane told me he had an out of body experience. He claims he watched as I gave him CPR. He was grateful for my helping him and thanked me profusely.”

“And the epiphany you mentioned? What realization did he have?” I queried.

“He told me he was going to get a divorce,” Barry shrugged.

“Any more information on that?” I asked.

“Nope. Whatever happened, it made him think that was what he should do. I think you are going to have your hands full with couples counseling.”

"I will conflicted, that is for certain. It might be best for me to refer them out to a priest in Mankato. She would be more comfortable with someone else."

"You don't think a divorce is the best thing?" Barry asked.

"No. I think maybe what he got was a wakeup call. If threatening a divorce gets him and his wife into counseling, it might reinforce for them the sanctity of their marriage."

"John, is there any terrible occurrence that you cannot find hope in?" Barry laughed.

"I always think of the hopelessness the Apostles felt on Good Friday. Yet that terrible thing renewed the world and gave us all life."

"When I grow up, I want to be just like you," Barry kidded me.

I put my hand on his shoulder.

"It is who I am. And, praise God, it is what I am called to do."

Barry gave me a funny look. Something more was on his mind.

"Speaking of being called to do something. We need to talk."

I felt like I was being called to the principal's office. The odd feeling I had was one of nervousness.

"I'm leaving," Barry told me.

I was stunned. All the plans I was making for Barry an hour ago were thrown out while I helplessly sat listening to him.

"Leaving?" I meekly asked.

"I am going back to Sliver City." Barry smiled as he shared his innermost feelings. "It became evident to me that I behaved cowardly at the Church of the Forsaken. Instead of cutting and running, I should have shown courage."

I wished I had the courage Barry was exhibiting now. He continued speaking.

"Jesus promised us not an easy life here on earth. Far from it. He did promise that he would be with us always. He was there to support me at Sliver City but I refused Him because things were not going the way I desired. I falsely discerned the narrative of how my life should proceed, so it was the only path I would accept. I coveted a certain life. When He did not do exactly what I demanded, I turned tail and ran. I have been foolish and cowardly. Instead of wondering why Jesus was not making my path a bed of roses, I should have been getting off my butt and pushing forward. The adventure of blazing my own trail beckoned to me, but I demanded an easy cruise down a smooth freeway.

The truth is I have squandered many of the opportunities He has given me."

"You have been a blessing to me and you will continue to be so in Sliver City," I said as I placed my hand on his shoulder. "I thank God for the time you have spent here. Mom and Carl will be sad to see you go, too."

Something prompted me to finish my thought.

"And John Paul. I think he has really gotten attached to you in a short time. Your presence seems to have made a difference in him. He seems more together these days. John Paul is unique. He always will be. He will miss you more than anyone."

"Uh, not really." Barry startled me with this comment.

"Why do you say that?" I asked, my innocence showing forth.

"Because John Paul is coming with me," Barry said.

My facial expression no doubt showed that I was stunned

"Coming with you?" I stammered.

"As John Paul and I got to know each other while we worked around the grounds, he opened up to me. It seems he is distanced from his family due to how they treated his older brother." Barry paused to make sure I was following.

"Go on, please," I requested.

"He admired his older brother. When his brother announced he was gay, everyone turned against him. He had to leave town and lost touch with the family. John Paul no longer had his older brother around for guidance. He resented his parents for the loss of his brother. Drugs and alcohol, as they do to many confused teenagers, became a way to deal with the emotional trauma. As he became more dependent on substances, his parents threw him out of the house, too. He has been wandering for the last several years. John Paul told me this is the first place where he has felt welcome since he left home."

"I am stunned, Barry."

"He and I have become friends. While he loves you and Carl – and especially Evie – he thinks it would be best to move to Sliver City with me. We will have the same arrangement as we do here. John Paul will work for room and board. Do you know he told me he hasn't used drugs since he moved in here? You should feel proud of what you have done for the man."

"Any good that happened isn't due to me, I'm sure. It is true what they say, God does work in mysterious ways. Still, I am surprised that as comfortable as he is here, he wants to move."

"I haven't told you the rest of the story."

Barry had my rapt attention. I could not imagine what else there could be to the story.

"John Paul believes it would make sense to live with me since I will be the one instructing him in the faith." Barry continued to stun me with every word that came out of his mouth.

"He's . . . what?" The words left my mouth in a scrambled fashion.

"John Paul said that he sees how Catholics treat people, even those who are different, as family. He told me he has never seen people treat strangers with such love. John Paul told me that any faith that embraces people like himself and me is the faith he wants to be a part of."

"Any faith that attracts people like you and John Paul," I said, "is the faith I want to be part of."

I embraced Barry. We made our way home.

A family meeting was held in the parish home that evening. It was one of the toughest gatherings I have ever been a part of. Emotions ran high. Tears were shed. We ended the meeting with laughter and joy. Carl led us in prayer. As we sat quietly after, Mom started singing "Amazing Grace." It was the sweetest song I had ever heard.

CHAPTER FIFTEEN

For once I had no reason to complain about my Bishop. He had telephoned me a respectful two days previously to ask that I meet him at his diocese office. Kevin told me that there would be a third person present, a representative from the Cardinal's office. There was nothing more he could tell me. This obvious sense of mystery put me a bit on edge, but Kevin assured me this was nothing that I needed to worry about.

I walked into the reception area and barely had time to sit down before Kevin came out to greet me. It had been a couple of months since we had seen each other. He looked tired. Like anyone our age he always looked a few pounds overweight, but today he looked thinner than I had ever seen him. I didn't have time to think much more about it because he introduced me to the third man in our meeting.

“Father John Krentz, I would like you meet Monsignor William Scalini, assistant to the Cardinal.”

“Very pleased to meet you, Monsignor.” I was as polite as I could be. My curiosity was overwhelming my senses, but I knew this was a situation where I had to sit tight and be patient.

We sat down and exchanged pleasantries about the Monsignor’s travel to Minnesota. This was a coming home of sorts for him as he grew up on the Iron Range of the state. After a short stint working in the mines he decided his vocation was serving God instead of digging iron ore. Since then he had served as a parish priest but found more of a calling for administration. His skills made him of great value to the Cardinal and the church in this part of the country.

The Monsignor made a short segue to turn the conversation over to the Bishop. Kevin looked at me a small smile came to his lips.

"Thank you, John, for coming here today. We have much to talk about."

I knew not to speak. Any words that left my lips would just delay things.

"We have a proposition for you. A major change in your life," he said with great calmness and effect.

"Well, change can be good," I admitted. "As you know, my life has changed considerably in the last year, and it has all been good."

It was clear to me I was going to be reassigned to a new parish. It made sense. I had been at St. Jude's for many years. One can become complacent by staying in the same place too long. As much as I loved the parishioners and the city, I accepted that priests seldom stayed in the same church as long as I had. I would embrace the new church and community. I hoped there would not be any problem with moving Mom with me. She would hate to leave her friends behind, but I was certain she would want to come with me. It all made sense. But there was one piece of my solved puzzle that did not fit. Why would the Monsignor be here? Surely the Bishop did not think I was such a hothead that he needed some support from a man of his status? No, something was amiss. I had a sinking feeling as I examined the Bishop's face. There was something gravely wrong. He confirmed my conclusion immediately.

"I am dying." Kevin spoke with noble serenity.

My personality was one where I attempted to control my emotions and not show any emotions. I am certain my face was now showing tremendous concern and sadness.

"I have cancer," he continued, placing a spike through my heart. "It is advanced. It's not much of a surprise, I guess. Half the people in my family have had cancer by the time they turned sixty. It is just some bad genetics."

"Your doctors, what do they say?" I was grasping at straws.

Kevin waved me quiet.

"We don't need to get into that. Yes, I have good doctors. Yes, they are doing everything they can. No, they do not hold out much hope. I am quite okay with that. This life has been very good to me, but we all know this is not my home. I belong with God. I just hope He will have me."

"Kev – " I bit my lip at this sign of disrespect in front of the Monsignor, "Bishop O'Reilly, I cannot begin to tell you how distressed this news makes me. Your leadership and holiness here has set an example for every priest in the diocese. I know working with me has never been easy, and I hope you know how much I appreciate all you have done."

“Thanks, John. I always considered our jousts a lot of fun. The best way to keep the boss on his toes is to stir the pot. Question everything – that is what Jesus told us.”

The Monsignor laughed. “Said by someone who knows of what he speaks.”

I was stunned by the implication.

“Bishop O’Reilly? Is there something behind the tranquil demeanor you always present to me?”

“John, to the priests I supervise I have to be a composed, mature figure. My position requires someone who can be that essential rock for them to rely on. The job of a Bishop is not just to provide spiritual leadership to the public. It is crucial to support the priests, take on their frustration, and let them air out their issues.”

“I am beginning to appreciate you all the more.” I hung my head down.

It was as quiet as if I were in the solitude of the forest. I looked up at the Bishop and then the Monsignor. Suddenly the sinking feeling I had minutes earlier grew more severe. I wondered if a rush for the door would be a good idea.

“John, we need to appoint someone in the interim to perform the duties of the Bishop of the Diocese. We need a strong leader, someone who has proven himself. Of course the final decision is not ours, it is solely the purview of his holiness, the Pope. Until he decides on who will fill the position permanently, we would like you to assume the position of Acting Bishop.”

“Declined! Declined with full respect, sirs.” I was as polite and as firm as I had ever been.

The Bishop glanced at the Monsignor with a "told you so" kind of look on his face.

"Declined?" the Monsignor asked. "May I ask why?"

"Monsignor, I am a parish priest. Where I am is where I belong. The job I have now is my dream. It is a perfect fit for me." I felt confident I was selling them my point of view.

"Monsignor, being from the state of Minnesota, you no doubt remember the term "Minnesota Nice." The people living here are reluctant to accept praise and in some cases, promotion. Don't you agree, John?" the Bishop explained.

"It is not that. I assure you." It was imperative I won this argument. Happily, I was certain my worthlessness would not be difficult to prove. The Bishop jumped feet first into the fray.

"John, let us be clear with the circumstances. Evie would be a breath of fresh air here. She would be an asset to the Diocese. I would insist you bring her with."

"Thank you. Still, I am not the person for the job. The fact is, I do not want the job and refuse to accept it."

The Monsignor was studying me carefully. I was upfront and honest. I had convinced myself there was nothing he would discover in me that I had not verbally put forth. Once again I was proven wrong.

"Very well then, Father. We certainly would not force you into something you do not want to do. Just one more question, if I may." A master had set his trap.

"Yes, of course," I answered, feeling that I had successfully made my escape.

“In one word, describe your current situation,” the Monsignor asked.

“Comfortable,” was the word that rushed from my lips. How I wished I could have pulled the sound back into my mouth before it bounced against their ears.

In all the meetings in all the years I had met with Kevin, I had seen many expressions during our conversations – various forms of upset, unhappiness, and sometimes a bit of anger. Never before had I seen a look of disappointment. His disappointment was not in my words, it was in my heart. It stung.

Nothing more could be said or done. I stood up and thanked them for the meeting. As I opened the door, the Bishop told me one more thing.

"John, the offer is good for twenty-four hours. I need to hear from you by four o'clock tomorrow as to your final decision. One way or another."

"Thank you, Bishop O'Reilly."

The longest drive I had ever experienced finally ended as I pulled into the drive at my home. Looking up into the sky, I couldn't tell if the clouds or the sun was going to rule the day. I realized it did not matter because the steeple of the church was so tarnished it couldn't reflect light anyway. I braked my car and sat there. A tear came out and rolled down my cheek. A ray of sun struck the water and I swear I saw a rainbow emerge from that small drop of fluid.

Not since I got my first car, a used hot rod, did I gun my accelerator so hard it spun my car around in a half circle. It wasn't smart or something I would have wanted anyone to see me doing, but I spun my car around and headed back out on the road. Pushing the speed limit, I cruised to town and the local hardware store. Within the hour I had returned. I ran into the house, barely acknowledging Carl and mom, both of whom were sitting in the living room.

With great haste I ran back outside, having first changed into a sweatshirt and old blue jeans. Pulling my car trunk open, I started pulling out tools, rope, buckets, scrubbing buckets and lots of cleaning fluids.

Mom and Carl came out and walked over to me. They had puzzled looks on their faces.

"Johnny, what in the world are you doing? How did the meeting with the Bishop go?" Mom was worried about me.

"The meeting went well. So well, in fact, that I just made a quick phone call to him. But we'll talk about that later tonight." There just was not any time to talk right now.

I grabbed a handful of working material and started walking towards the church.

"John," Carl said, "you did not answer Evie's question. What are you doing?"

"Pull up some lawn chairs and watch me," I stated with a growing feeling of joy. "I am going to clean the church steeple."

THE END

Made in the USA
Charleston, SC
15 July 2015